The Hole Truth

Inside the Ropes of the PGA Tour

Bruce Nash and Allan Zullo
with George White

ANDREWS and McMEEL
A Universal Press Syndicate Company
Kansas City

Designed by Barrie Maguire

Library of Congress Cataloging-in-Publication Data
Nash, Bruce M.
     The hole truth : inside the ropes of the PGA tour /
Bruce Nash and Allan Zullo with George White.
     p.   cm.
     ISBN: 0-8362-7029-0
     1. Professional Golfers' Association of America.
2. PGA Tour (Association)   3. Golf—Tournaments—
United States.   I. Zullo, Allan. II. White, George,
     1945–   . III. Title.
GV970.N37   1995
796.352'66—dc20   94–49577
                                                                    CIP

Dedication

To Alan Berger, for your encouragement,
support, and friendship.
—*Bruce Nash*

To Il Conte Giacomo and La Contessa Marcella Berghini,
whose class off the course far outshines their skills on it.
—*Allan Zullo*

Contents

Acknowledgments

We wish to thank all the Tour pros who graciously consented to be surveyed and interviewed.

We are grateful to the team of reporters who so professionally carried out our surveys, including Mike Jamison, Bruce Stephen, and especially George White, veteran golf writer and Golf Channel analyst, without whose assistance we couldn't have completed this book.

We also appreciate the help of noted golf reporter Robinson Holloway, who provided us with the results of several recent polls she conducted with the pros on such subjects as the best and worst tournaments and the most and least popular playing partners.

Also, we relied on some background material published in *Golfweek*, *Golf Digest*, and *Golf* magazines.

Inside the Ropes

Like a duffer's shot off the tee, life on the PGA Tour can twist and turn in many directions. Rookies have burst on the scene from out of nowhere to capture a major; others have disappeared in the bunkers of fate. Talented pros have spent years working their way up onto the leaderboard of superstars; other veterans have played for over a decade on the Tour and never won—and never even finished second. Yet even the winless still can claim to be among the best one hundred golfers in the world.

The road that the pros must travel to reach the PGA Tour is an arduous one that goes through Qualifying School. Rookies can't play with the big boys on the Tour until they prove their skill and mettle. And if a veteran doesn't earn enough money on the Tour during the year, he must qualify all over again, just like a rookie. Play well in the Q School finals and you get your coveted Tour card, allowing you to compete against the top players in the game with hundreds of thousands dollars up for grabs every week. Play poorly and you're stuck in the low-rent mini-tours against guys you know aren't nearly as good as you.

Not everyone makes it on the first try. Curtis Strange bogeyed the last three holes in the final round to miss qualifying by one shot. "I remember doubting myself, wondering if I really had what it took to play on the Tour," he once recalled. The following spring, he earned his card and proved to himself—and everyone else—that he definitely had what it takes.

The PGA Tour sounds glamorous, but the players will tell you it's more grind than glamour. It's called the Tour for a reason. The player becomes an urban nomad, constantly on the road, from January through August, and often into October. "We do go to beautiful places," says veteran Scott Simpson, "but we do our own laundry, don't always stay in the nicest places, and we have to travel."

As soon as he holes out on the 18th on Sunday, the typical pro packs up his gear and heads to a different town. On Monday, he appears at a corporate outing, giving a clinic and playing a few holes with the amateurs. If he's lucky, the outing is near the next tournament; otherwise, he has to hop a plane.

On Tuesday, he arrives at the tourney site and squeezes in a practice round to get familiar with the course. Wednesday is pro-am day, when he plays with eighteen-handicappers and tries to be sociable to strangers who've forked over a couple of grand for the privilege of having him as their playing partner.

The tournament begins on Thursday. By Friday afternoon, he learns whether or not he's made the cut. A bad score and he leaves empty-handed. His reward for shooting a good score is that he doesn't get to go home for the weekend. On Saturday, he tees off, knowing he's guaranteed a paycheck. A victory can mean pocketing more bucks in four days than a decent teacher makes in eight years. A finish near the bottom can mean earning barely enough to meet expenses.

And then it's back on the plane or in the car and the cycle starts all over again, playing golf not for fun but to pay the bills.

When the pros do make it home, most are forced to practice. They do it out of fear—fear that their competitors are back home practicing harder than they are. So they kiss their kids and wife and head out to the practice range to whack a few hundred balls.

What PGA veteran Frank Beard said years ago still holds true today: "The Tour is not what most people seem to think. It's not all sunshine and pretty girls and cheering crowds. It's life without roots. It's a potentially rewarding life, but also a frustrating life. There's no real opponent except your own stupid mental and physical mistakes."

The competition is fierce. The only major difference between the top money winners and those in the middle of the money list, says Lee Janzen, "is the guys at the top know they are going to play well and the guys around seventieth just *hope* they will."

It's tough enough dealing with slick greens, tall rough, cruel pin placements, tricky winds, bad lies, and gallery loudmouths. The pro must also wage a constant battle with himself.

Davis Love III describes it this way: "The ball doesn't move. . . . It sits there on perfectly conditioned fairways. It's a brand-new golf ball we get for free, we're using brand-new equipment, we're [wearing] brand-new clothes that we get for free, and that ball sits there and says, 'Now, idiot, don't hit me in the hazard. Don't hit me over there, hit me on the green. You think you can, idiot? I doubt if you can. Especially when you're choking your guts out.' All these things go through your head because it takes three or four minutes between each shot.

"You and you alone are responsible for every shot. You need an imagination to figure out how you're going to get the ball from point A to point B within your abilities. You're by yourself and there's an awful lot of opportunities out there and a lot of ways to screw up."

The pressure the pro must handle and the mind games

he must play within himself often leach out the pure fun of the sport enjoyed by the weekend hacker.

Wrote noted columnist Tom Boswell, "If we don't count Lee Trevino and 7.3 other human beings this century, it's safe to say that it is impossible for a pro to play his best golf and enjoy himself at the same time. If he smiles, he'll bogey the next hole. Laugh, and it'll be a double. If he actually tells a joke to the crowd, he'll probably sign an incorrect card and be DQ'ed."

No matter how great the professional golfer is, he can never master the game—and he knows it. The top winners one year often find themselves tumbling dozens of spots below fellow golfers on the money list the next year.

But, hey, it's a living—and a lucrative one at that. The top dozen on the money list pocketed each over $700,000 in winnings in 1994. The fortieth man, Mike Heinen, made more than $390,000. David Feherty, who finished one hundredth on the list, still earned over $178,000. And these figures don't include endorsements, corporate outings, speeches, exhibitions, foreign events, charity functions, and other sources for fattening the player's wallet.

When you play five or six rounds a week for thirty or more weeks, there are days when you would rather do something else; days when the ball goes everywhere but where you want it to go; days when the fire and desire in your belly seem doused by complacency. But you go out there anyway because that's your job.

What keeps the average pro going, knowing that there are only so many tournaments to play and that the superstars are going to win the majority of them? A dream that things will get better; a hope that *this* is the tournament he'll win; the belief that he has yet to reach his full potential, that there's still plenty of room for improvement; and the anticipation of experiencing the sheer unadulterated pleasure of hitting the perfect shot.

The Hole Truth presents a slice of life on the PGA Tour as told by the players themselves in interviews and surveys conducted in the clubhouse, on the putting green, and at the 19th hole. Their comments and insights provide us with verbal snapshots of what it's like inside the gallery ropes: Fuzzy Zoeller whistling to relieve tension on the course . . . Corey Pavin saying a little prayer before attempting a clutch putt . . . Steve Pate learning to control his fiery temper . . . Paul Azinger surreptitiously shooting a squirt gun at the gallery . . . Nolan Henke perfecting the art of negative thinking . . . Nick Price entering "The Zone" . . . Lanny Wadkins doubling the bet during a practice round . . . and every player claiming he wouldn't trade this life for anything else in the world.

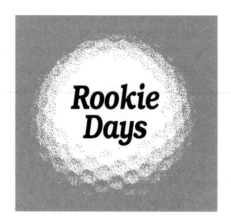

The Rookie Year

Pro Kelly Gibson has some fond memories—and a few mortifying ones—of his first year on tour in 1992.

"I once used the ladies' locker room not once but twice at the Phoenix Open in my rookie year," he confessed. "The first time I didn't realize I was in the wrong place. But the second time, as I was sitting there in the stall tending to the matter at hand, I suddenly heard a pair of high heels in the bathroom. When the coast was clear, I looked around and then I realized I was in the wrong place."

As a rookie, Gibson admitted he felt awed by the greats of the game.

"My brother Keith was caddying for me at the International in my rookie year. We were eating breakfast [two days before the tournament] when suddenly Greg Norman walked over and asked me if I had a practice game lined up. I almost shit. I stalled for a moment and Keith started kicking me under the table as if to say, 'Take it, take it.'

"So I went out and played the practice round with Greg. I couldn't breathe for the first thirty minutes, I was trying so hard to impress him. And I didn't introduce Greg to Keith, who is a doctor in real life. I was just treating him like a regular caddie. Finally, my brother came over to me and said, 'If you don't introduce me to him, I'm going to drop your bag on the ground and walk off right now.' Greg overheard Keith and came over and introduced himself, with a look of amusement on his face. He had no idea Keith was my brother and my doctor."

The first year on the Tour is tough, says Gibson. "For rookies, it's a grinding, grinding year. In most cases, you're going to tournaments you've never played in before. The cities are new and the courses are new to you. You don't know where to stay or where to eat. You don't have a travel routine down. You don't know how to practice. It's a bitch. The second year goes much better.

"One time in my rookie year, I flew into Miami International Airport for the Doral. The course is only fifteen minutes from the airport. But I made one wrong turn and it took me two hours to find my way to the course."

What do you remember about the first time you were in contention in a Tour event?

Billy Andrade: "I threw up all over myself. I know I felt very nervous, not knowing what to expect next. I was real antsy knowing I had to play well to win. It was a feeling I'd never had."

John Cook: "I was leading in Boston in my rookie year, and the adrenaline was pumping so hard I hit a wedge twenty yards over the green and made a seven. I kind of deflated after that."

Lee Janzen: "It was at Hattiesburg my first year. I was pretty nervous, and started hitting it all over the place. I somehow scraped it in from everywhere and finished fifth."

Jim Gallagher Jr.: "It was in Memphis in 1984, my first year. I choked my guts out. I was as nervous as a cat on a hot tin roof and shot 76."

Influence Peddlers

When the pros were asked who inspired them the most early in their careers, here's what they had to say:

Fulton Allem: "There's no doubt in my mind that Gary Player has been the greatest inspiration in my life. He has been the spark within me that has pushed me to whatever I am. I owe it all to him."

Allem grew up in South Africa, where his father owned a fifty thousand–acre ranch. "I was friends with Fulton's father and uncle," recalled Player. "I had just won the British Open and I wanted a place to go have a rest. So they invited me to the ranch and we played golf."

One day Player saw five-year-old Fulton hacking around with his grandfather's left-handed clubs. The boy looked up at the South African star and said that some day he would beat Player.

"Player laughed and then told me, 'If you're going to do that, you're going to have to stand on the other side of the ball,'" recalled Allem. "Then he went out and bought me my first set of clubs—right-handed ones."

With encouragement and tips from Player, Allem decided to make a career out of golf.

"I really don't think I can take much credit for Fulton's success," says Player. "It's nice to hear that I have been a motivation for him, but I don't want to diminish the hard work that he has put into his golf game."

Chip Beck: "William O'Donnell, a good friend, made a big impact on my life. I thought I was going to become a Catholic priest. Toward the end of my senior year in college, I didn't think golf had any altruistic value to it. It seemed like a selfish endeavor.

"And then I met William O'Donnell in 1977. Right afterward, I got a letter from him. It changed my life."

The letter, which Beck has kept at his home, said, in part, "Golf is a science that if perfected can change your life and the life of thousands of others. One need not look farther than Arnold Palmer, Sam Snead, or Ben Hogan to understand my point. . . . Golf is a wholesome sport that demands a saintlike spirit. One's strength, wit, honor, compassion, and self-love grow with each shot of every round. . . . I ask you to stop and reflect on your life, the good people you have met, the competition and the winning. Chip, there can be no doubt as to the importance of golf in your life. . . ."

Beck said that the letter was critical in his decision to forgo the priesthood for a career in golf.

Raymond Floyd: "Arnold Palmer was my hero. To see him with those late charges, tugging at those pants, that was something. He wasn't my mentor but he set an example for me.

"I never took a golf lesson from Arnold, but I took a million playing lessons. Back in the mid-1960s, I played a lot of practice rounds with Arnold. I searched for him at tournaments. I'd find out when he was practicing—daylight or dark, I didn't care. 'Arnold, where do you like to drive it on this hole?' I'd ask. That one question would open up a world of explanation.

"I watched the way he handled the courses and handled his game. I tried to emulate his aggressive style of play. I owe Arnold a great deal. He still calls me 'Sonny' and I like that."

Curtis Strange: "I'll never forget the time my father told me, 'Never say you can't do it.' I was bitching and moaning about my grip. I said I couldn't do it the way he wanted me to. And he looked at me and said, 'Don't you ever say that. You can do anything you want to do. I don't ever want to hear you say that again.' That has always stayed with me. I guess it helped make me tough inside."

Fuzzy Zoeller: "Arnold Palmer was the number-one guy on TV and I was inspired by him. To this day, I owe a lot to Arnold and to Jack Nicklaus. But Arnold's the one who did more for me—as far as attitude and how to treat people and react to people—than any other golfer."

Nick Faldo visited the great Ben Hogan
to ask the master for a tip on how
to win the U.S. Open.
"What you have to do," said the
always cool Hogan,
"is shoot the lowest score."

The Pressure Cooker

Battle of Nerves

Most every pro admits he gets scared on the course.

"Do you want to know the definition of scary?" asks Mark O'Meara. "Scary is standing in the middle of the fairway with a seven-iron in your hand and having no idea whether you can hit the green or what the shot is going to do. That's scary."

"I get nervous," admits Fred Couples. "I might not show it, but I do. What people see, I guess, is that I'm a slow swinger and I walk slow and people think that means I'm lackadaisical."

Raymond Floyd says that he's been scared of certain shots. "I fear shots when I'm uncertain about them. There are shots where, for some reason, I start getting negative thoughts. And when that happens, sure, I get scared.

"For example, there's the tee shot on the 5th hole at the Colonial in Texas where I fear I might push the ball into the creek. There's the tee shot at the final hole at Doral where I might pull or hook into the lake."

Lee Janzen, known for his mental toughness, needed plenty of it at the 1993 U.S. Open to carry the burden of leading from the thirtieth hole on. Janzen, who won the Open by two strokes, recalled that on the day of the final round, "I woke up with a knot in my stomach and it didn't go away all day."

While chasing Greg Norman in the 1993 PGA Championship, Paul Azinger recalled that over the last few holes, he fought hard to keep his nerves under control. "After the 16th hole, I questioned myself on whether I was going to be able to perform. I asked, 'Am I going to throw up? What am I going to do?' It just put a little more pressure on me. And I felt every bit of that pressure."

He settled down and birdied the 17th hole to set up a playoff with Norman. "At the end of the round, I was gasping for air," Azinger said. "It was as much pressure as I've ever felt." Azinger, who kept taking deep breaths to relax, nipped Norman on the second playoff hole to capture the PGA Championship.

Ian Baker-Finch was leading after three rounds of the 1984 British Open and was paired with Tom Watson for the final round. But Baker-Finch fell victim to nerves and plunked his approach shot into the drink on the 1st hole and quickly faded to a nightmarish 79.

"I had to fight to keep the tears out of my eyes," he recalled. "For me, it was a dream come true to play the final round with Watson, but it was difficult. I was so apprehensive. You start feeling a lot of emotion out there. You start feeling like you screwed up and you're wondering what everyone is thinking. And you're thinking that the whole of Australia is sitting up watching you shoot 79. I felt I had failed."

Payne Stewart admits he didn't handle pressure situations too well in the past because of fear, but he relishes them now.

In the mid-1980s, Stewart had a tendency to fritter away leads late in the final round. He needed to learn how to better handle these pressure-packed moments. So he visited Dr. Richard Coop, a University of North Carolina professor who counsels athletes.

"Losing like I did, it was just an inability to deal with the situations," Stewart admitted. "Dr. Coop said I was scared to hit the shot that could win it all because it might be the one that loses it all."

Dr. Coop told him to use a preshot routine every time he was about to address the ball. Such repetition helped give Stewart security. Then the professor planted in the golfer's mind the thought that Thursday's first shot was just as important as Sunday's last putt. That way, Stewart wouldn't feel more pressure on one shot than on another.

Dr. Coop also noticed that Stewart's tendency to falter from the 15th hole on indicated a possible metabolism problem that could adversely affect his swing and his judgment. So Stewart began eating a banana late in the round.

After a four-year winning drought, Stewart won the Hertz Bay Hill Classic in 1987 and later the PGA Championship in 1989 and the U.S. Open in 1991 among other tournaments.

"Now I thrive on pressure situations," says Stewart. "Just get me in that situation. I'm not scared of the moment."

Tom Kite believes that the best golfers are the ones who play scared.

"When people see a guy coming down the stretch, trying to win a golf tournament, he looks so calm and so collected. He looks like everything is under control. What they don't understand is that the guy is not calm. He may have learned how to control his emotions, but I can assure you he is not calm.

"No matter how many times you win, the nervousness is there—and it's great. That's the best thing about it—to put yourself in that position and to get nervous, to really get scared. It's what it's all about.

"People don't understand how wonderful that feeling is to be absolutely scared to death. And then you pull the shots off. It is an incredible feeling. Being scared, that's fun. That's good.

"When my kids play sports, the one thing I want them to really appreciate is how important being nervous is and what a great benefit it is. It's what allows people to do superhuman things.

"If you're not scared, if you don't have that adrenaline pumping, all you can do is average things. If you're not scared, it means you don't care."

The next time you see a player in a pressure situation, says Kite, don't think, "The guy is scared so he probably won't do any good." Instead, think, "The guy is scared so he will probably do great."

Kite suffered a totally humiliating collapse under pressure at the 1989 U.S. Open.

After taking the third-round lead, Kite told reporters, "A lot of people who entered this tournament don't have the opportunity to be scared to death tomorrow. I anticipate it. I welcome it. I want to be nervous. Do I have total control? Nah. Neither does anybody else. It's you against yourself and you hope you can stand up to it."

But a triple bogey and two double bogies finished him off. "It's a bitter pill to swallow," he said afterward. "To have a chance to win and perform the way I did. That's by far my worst round."

Hale Irwin said he must wage a constant battle with himself to maintain composure and confidence in pressure situations. "You're completely alone, with every conceivable opportunity to defeat yourself. What really matters is resiliency. There's going to come a time when you want to throw yourself into the nearest trash can and disappear.

"It's like you're walking down the fairway naked. The gallery knows what you've done, every other player knows, and worst of all, you know."

Peter Jacobsen, who has yet to win a major, imagines how it might feel to stand over a shot that could win his first major: "Am I going to have the guts to stand in there and hit the best shot I can and accept the consequences? All those practice shots don't mean a thing. You have to be able to stand on the last hole and say, 'It's due right now.' And then perform."

Strange said he choked once—and has been determined never to do it again.

"I choked at the first qualifying school I went to in Brownsville, Texas," he recalled. "I choked my guts out, and it hurt so much I didn't ever want to do it again. I've won some and lost some, but I've never been that out of control since.

"I'm not going to blow a tournament. They're going to have to beat me. I'm as nervous as anybody else, and I have as much anxiety. But the key is, I enjoy that feeling and I can still concentrate.

"Playing well when the heat is on—that's when you find out how well you can play. Every time you come down the stretch, you're going to have to hit a shot or make a putt. Nothing makes me feel better than to hit a clutch shot.

"I never thought I was the most talented person in the world, so I had to succeed in other areas. You know, confidence, inner strength, and the ability to handle my emotions at all times. I've lost my temper, lost control at times, but never when the heat is on. When it's crunch time, I've always been in control."

Brad Bryant says he doesn't feel the same kind of pressure that the top money winners feel. "I haven't had that many shots under a lot of pressure because," he adds with a smile, "the others play better than I do."

However, Bryant believes that the players in the back of the pack experience their own kind of pressure. "The shot to me that's really pressure is when you're not playing well and you're trying to make the cut," he said. "When you're near the lead, you're probably swinging and playing well. I don't feel a lot of pressure from the standpoint of hitting a bad shot.

"But when you're right on the cut number and you're hitting the ball all over the place and you've got to make par on the last hole to make the cut, now you're choking your guts out. All you're trying to do is hit the ball in the fairway instead of trying to make a good swing. Suddenly you've got rubber coming out from between your fingers. I have hit the ugliest dog putt when I was simply trying to two-putt to make the cut. It looked like I threw the ball down there and then threw up on it to make it stop."

The Very Definition of Pressure

Here's how Dan Forsman describes the pressure of the Masters:

"Put a two-by-four over two cinder blocks six feet apart and you can walk across it—no problem. But put a two-by-four over the top of the World Trade Center and have the wind blowing and people lining up waiting for your demise and roaring here and there and having read all about the ones who have gone through there and fallen to their deaths and then try to walk across *that*.

"That's the pressure I feel. That gives you an idea of just what it's about."

The Nightmare of Q School

Of all the pressures pro golfers face, nothing is quite like the PGA Qualifying School.

Golfers need to pass the rigorous and stressful Q School in order to get a Tour card for the year if they're rookies or if they were Tour players who failed to make it on the list of the top 125 money winners for the previous year. Nearly a thousand golfers a year vie in regional and district tournaments for the chance to make it to the grinding, six-day qualifying finale. The top forty-five get to play on the PGA Tour.

"It's unlike any other pressure you will ever feel playing this sport," says Gary Koch, an eighteen-year veteran. "I've represented the United States on Walker Cup teams, world amateur teams, I've won on the Tour, and I've been in contention in major tournaments.

"The difference is, at Tour School, you're playing for your future, for your livelihood. It's your one opportunity, and you don't get another shot at it for another year."

Even if you pass, the experience is so stressful that pros experience nightmares about it for years.

Donnie Hammond, who has earned over two million dollars on the PGA Tour, has gone through Q School three times. "Each time it was the most pressure I could imagine, not just in golf, but in anything I've done in life," he said.

"Each time before Q School, I'd have nightmares. I'd dream that I only played three holes and already I was five over par. It was such an emotional dream I would wake myself up. Then I'd realize I was in my bed and the tournament hadn't even started yet. I'd shout, 'Great! I'm back at even par!'"

Mark McCumber, who has earned over $3.2 million on the PGA Tour, said he still is haunted by a recurring dream of Q School even though he gained his card way back in 1978—after failing to qualify his first three times.

"In my dream, I shoot an 82 in the last round and I go to the scorer's tent in disgust and fling my scorecard down without bothering to sign it. Next, I go to the parking lot, sit on the trunk of my car with my head in my hands, totally disgusted with myself.

"Then someone asks how I did and I say bitterly, 'I shot an 82 to finish two under. The person says, 'Hey, two under is going to make it!' I tear back to the scorer's tent, scrambling to find my card. Then I run to the tournament official, telling him I haven't left the property yet, begging him to let me sign my card. That's when I wake up. So tell me Tour school didn't affect me."

David Peoples went through Tour School nine times. Six times he earned his card only to fail to make enough money to keep it the following year. "I could always get through the school," said Peoples, "but I could never make enough money to keep my card. People used to always tell me, 'Once you get through school, you've got it made.' Yeah, right." Three times he failed to qualify, and each time it knocked the emotional props out from under him.

"You invest all of your life into something, since you were a kid, then you can't get through the school," he said.

"Now you're trying to be honest with yourself. 'Well, should I do something else? This is what I've been working for all my life, to be a professional golfer, and this one dog-gone tournament is keeping me from doing it.' "

For those who miss the final cut, the sudden attack of self-doubt can make a man wonder why he ever tried in the first place. "It makes you feel like, 'You're not good enough, son, for this line of work,' " said McCumber. "You feel like a snotball, if I can be so crude."

Pro Larry Rinker missed qualifying three times by one measly shot before finally succeeding in 1981. They still talk about the time future pro Bob Tway ballooned to an 83 on the final day in 1982, missing his card by two strokes.

As horrifying as Tour School can be, it's a week that every PGA Tour player should never forget, says pro Russ Cochran. "We on the Tour need to refresh our memories about what that experience was like. There is nothing else in sports that is even close to it. In reality, it's the essence of our game."

When Larry Gilbert went through the Senior PGA Tour Qualifying School before the 1993 season, he admitted having a severe case of the nerves. Said Gilbert, "I kept telling my wife Brenda that I haven't been this nervous since I lost my virginity. And she said, 'That was with me, wasn't it?'"

What is the most intimidating situation in competitive golf?

Fulton Allem: "Needing to hole a six-footer to win."

Tom Kite: "Trying to win a major, I guess. Really, there's nothing out here that's that scary."

Lee Janzen: "Anytime you've got a severe sidehill lie and you can't ground the club."

Joey Sindelar: "I hate to state the obvious, but trying to play a tough golf course with no golf swing."

Ernie Els: "When you have to make two birdies on the last two holes and you're not hitting that good. Or you have to do it to make the cut."

Hal Sutton: "Going into Amen Corner at Augusta with a one-shot lead, that would be pretty intimidating. You'd want to be there, of course, but it's a tough spot to be in."

"The game embarrasses you until you feel inadequate and pathetic. You want to cry like a child."

—Ben Crenshaw

How do you relax in pressure-packed situations on the course?

Paul Azinger: "I do some form of breathing exercises during a pressure situation. It definitely helps. Every time, before I hit a key shot, I take a deep breath and cleanse the mind."

Larry Rinker: "In addition to taking some deep breaths, I take a moment to look at the scenery and then I tell myself, 'I'm happy to be here.'"

Payne Stewart: "I rehearse in my mind what I am going to do and I tell myself that I have hit this shot before. The best thing I can do in such a situation is think positive thoughts."

Donnie Hammond: "I think about puppy dogs and my kids. I try to picture myself in a Jacuzzi in Palm Springs at night and I remember how relaxed I was when I gazed up at the stars. I try to ignore all the people around me who are waiting for me to hit the ball. Then I tell myself, 'Well, you've screwed up so many times in the past, who cares if you do it one more time? On the other hand, you've screwed up so often, why don't you do something good for a change?'"

David Peoples: "I try to put the tense moment in perspective. Sometimes I just think about how insignificant it really is with all the rest of the things going on in the world. When I get so nervous that I'm physically impeded, I'll just think about how many people are starving and that they could care less about this shot."

Fuzzy Zoeller: "I like to whistle to relieve tension. Also, I don't concentrate when I'm walking down that fairway. I think Jack Nicklaus has been the only one who has mastered the art of concentrating for eighteen straight holes. You have to have that little out, give yourself a little break and then get back into it. So I do anything I can to relax. I whistle or talk to my playing partners or say something to the crowd. I try to focus only when I pull the club out of the bag."

Bill Murchison: "Preparation is the key to lessening the pressure. Most things that need to be done to reduce pressure should be done prior to the tournament. It's basic stuff like knowing beforehand exactly where you want to hit the ball and how to play each shot. Once I'm on the course, it's important to remember to slow down. Golfers tend to hurry under pressure. I make it very clear in my mind what I want to do. For example, I tell myself, 'I want to start this shot over the little pine and fade it toward the pin.' It helps under pressure to really state exactly what you want to do."

Mark McCumber: "I talk a lot, especially to the gallery. Some fan will say something or a baby will cry and I'll back off and make a comment that relieves a lot of tension for me. The key to relieving tension is to be yourself. If a guy is quiet, he needs to stay quiet. If a guy is, by nature, emotional and talkative like me, he needs to let that out."

Grant Waite: "To relax, I try to walk a little slower and take nice deep breaths. I like to focus on a stationary object like a tree because when I'm nervous, I tend to golf too fast, so this slows me down."

Mike Hulbert: "I just don't let pressure situations bother me. I realize that if I miss the shot, it's not the end of the world. I tell myself to do the best I can and then I don't worry any more about it."

Comedy Clubs

Pro golfer JC Andersen—the unknown comic on the PGA Tour—says laughter is the greatest tonic for releasing tension on the course.

"I see humor in any situation, even if I'm choking my guts out," he said.

If he blows a shot, he just starts laughing—and gets others to laugh along with him. "It's better than getting bent out of shape," he explained. "I love making people laugh.

"Laughter is the only way to go. Heck, I've gone to a half-dozen sports psychologists. Each time, they gave me my money back and told me to go to another guy and drive *him* crazy."

In two years on the Tour, Andersen has achieved more notoriety with his one-liners than with his clubs. At the 1993 Kemper Open, he had his best finish ever—sixth place. His check for $46,000 doubled his career earnings to date.

"I wasn't even in the top sixty in caddie earnings before the Kemper," Andersen said. "I'm serious. I'd go up to caddies and say, 'Can I borrow twenty dollars for the day?'"

■

During a pro-am in Boston, Fuzzy Zoeller relaxed on the first tee by relying on a little humor at the announcer's expense.

The course announcer told the gallery, "Next on the tee is a golfer who won the 1979 Masters and the 1984 U.S. Open. He was on three Ryder Cup teams. . . ."

While the introduction continued, Zoeller stepped up to the tee and blasted the ball straight down the middle of the fairway. Then, while the announcer was still talking, Zoeller shouted with tongue in cheek, "Would you shut up while I'm hitting?" The crowd roared and Zoeller laughed. The relaxed golfer finished among the top five.

■

Blaine McCallister needs to be relaxed to play his best. But his emotions sometimes make him too intense to perform at his optimum level.

His wife Claudia came up with a solution to make him relax. She told him, "Whenever you make a bogey, find the nearest marshal and give him a hug."

The first time McCallister tried her suggestion was at the 1993 H-E-B Texas Open. He hugged a startled marshal and went from a 74 in the third round to a much-improved 65 in the final round.

The following week, at the Las Vegas Invitational, McCallister was the second-round coleader when he was asked by a reporter if the golfer had hugged any marshals that day. "Nope," replied McCallister. "Claudia is with me this week and I hugged her once today. I guess she decided to keep an eye on me."

Blocking Out the Pressure

Beta blockers—commonly used to treat high blood pressure and anxiety—are used by some players on the Tour.

Former pro Mac O'Grady claims that some of the game's top players are unethically using beta blockers to calm their nerves in tournament play. He estimated that seven of the top thirty players in the world are abusing them.

O'Grady admitted taking beta blockers to relax in 1986. The PGA Tour does not have a policy against beta blockers because they are a prescription drug.

Nick Price said he used beta blockers for eight years because of high blood pressure. He added they weren't used to help him relax on the course. "Actually, they did more harm than good," he said. Beta blockers sapped him of energy and caused him many restless nights. "But in my case, it was either take medication or die."

Price said that when he switched from beta blockers to a different medication in 1988, he felt so much better that he began winning on the Tour.

"We all choke. You just try to choke last."

—Tom Watson

Playing Partners

Pairing Up

In most cases, it doesn't much matter with whom a Tour player is paired. Sometimes, however, pairings can affect a player's performance and indicate how much he'll enjoy his workday.

In polls conducted in 1993 and 1994, forty-five pros revealed who made the best and worst playing partners, and why.

Who are the most desirable playing partners?

Joey Sindelar
Nick Price
Fred Couples
Rocco Mediate
Lanny Wadkins
John Huston
Arnold Palmer

The best partners are congenial, positive-thinking golfers, like Joey Sindelar and Nick Price, who were mentioned most often as a favorite to play with. "You can't not like those guys," says John Cook.

The worst are those players who are either slow on the course, have unpleasant personalities, practice gamesmanship, or attract a rowdy gallery.

Interestingly, two-time Player of the Year Fred Couples made both the best and worst lists. Although he's popular with his fellow golfers, they're not fond of his slow play and the unruly galleries he attracts.

Who are the least favorite playing partners because of . . .

. . . slow play?

Chip Beck
Bob Estes
Larry Mize
Bernhard Langer
Fred Couples

. . . unruly galleries?

John Daly
Greg Norman
Fred Couples

. . . personality?

Hale Irwin
Nick Faldo
Scott Hoch
Ken Green

. . . gamesmanship?

Steve Elkington
Seve Ballesteros

Chip Beck earned the dubious distinction of being mentioned most often as the least desirable partner, primarily because of his slow play (which he has picked up since the poll was taken). Ironically, Beck is well liked among his peers. It's just that they don't want to play with him. "He's a nightmare," confided one pro. "He's the nicest guy in the world. I can't figure out how you can be so nice and so slow."

However, many players enjoy being paired with Beck because he's always complimenting his opponents when they make a good shot.

"I play well with Chip," says Ted Schulz. "His self-talk is just so positive, it rubs off on you. He can hit a really horrible shot and afterward talk so well to himself."

Beck's sunny attitude was seen as a negative by one quibbler, who noted that "while I'm ordinarily even-tempered and tough to rile, Chip is so happy he makes me grumpy."

Other players mentioned as bothersomely slow are Larry Mize, D.A. Weibring, Bernhard Langer, Mark Brooks, Dan Forsman, Bob Estes, Fred Couples, and Ray Floyd.

One fast player explains why slow play can go beyond maddening and become damaging: "When you're playing well, you don't notice it. But when you're borderline, and your concentration is off, it's all you see."

Almost as annoying as slow play is a bad attitude. The leaders in this class are Hale Irwin and Nick Faldo.

"I hate playing with guys like Hale who whine and moan," says one player. "I hate hearing guys bellyaching and throwing clubs, especially someone who has won three U.S. Opens."

Added another pro, "Hale is an absolute pain in the neck to play with. All he thinks of is himself: 'Did you see the bad bounce I got?' We all say it once in a while, but he's awful."

Said a third player who's not too fond of playing with

Irwin, "If he's putting bad, and someone in his group makes a few putts in a row, watch Hale when the other guy's putt goes in. He'll throw his arms up in disgust."

Larry Rinker says he's irked when his playing partner acts out his frustration over a bad game. "I don't like it when he loses it and doesn't give me any courtesy. He's always in a hurry to finish the hole and doesn't want to wait for the other guy. It's a real problem when your playing partner is doing poorly and just kind of gives up. He wants to haul butt around the course. It can affect you and cause you to rush. He can get you out of your own game. That can be pretty discourteous."

Who are the least talkative playing partners?

Nick Faldo
Bob Estes
Willie Wood
David Edwards
Jeff Maggert

Nick Faldo is known for giving his playing partners the silent treatment. "He won't even say 'good shot,'" complains one pro. "Faldo maintains a detached aloofness from almost everyone on tour."

Few things bother Ian Baker-Finch more than a playing partner like Faldo who won't smile. "I don't think it's right if I say 'good shot' to someone all day and he still ignores you," said the Australian.

"I don't mind playing with Nick," says Mark McCumber, "but he's extremely quiet. Most quiet guys still will acknowledge when you make a good shot. But Nick is in his zone and he doesn't even know you are there. In fact, if you holed out a two-iron, you probably won't even get a nod from him."

Brad Bryant agrees. "Faldo doesn't say anything. He doesn't even watch you. He's off in another world."

Nick Price is the exact opposite of Faldo. "Nick's [Faldo] priorities in life are very different from mine and a lot of other people's," says Price. "We all have self-centered priorities as players, but we still have a little bit of time for other things. I have been close to Nick in times gone by and he can be a very friendly person. But he has just adopted this attitude [of aloofness on the course]. One day, he may regret it. You've got trophies and a huge bank balance, but, hey, that doesn't make friends."

Who are the most talkative playing partners?

Scott Hoch
Peter Jacobsen
Mark McCumber
Lee Trevino
Fuzzy Zoeller
Jay Delsing
Ed Dougherty

At the other extreme, endless chatter is a sure route to alienating fellow competitors. Scott Hoch is the undisputed champion of gab. "He's a nice guy, but he never shuts up," said one golfer.

Negative thinking is another irritating trait. Says one player, "You can get caught up in a playing partner's negativeness. If he keeps saying, 'the greens are bad, the greens are bad,' you start wondering if the greens *are* bad."

Bryant says he's bothered by playing partners who are

constantly complaining. "They gripe all day long. But if they're bothering me, that's my fault because I've let them bother me rather than concentrate on my game."

Other players are so self-absorbed they don't notice when they are distracting their partners. They might be so engrossed in planning their next shot that they don't realize they are moving while their playing partner is about to swing. Mark Calcavecchia and Ken Green were cited by several pros for such actions, although none of those polled felt it was deliberate.

Payne Stewart says he gets irritated by partners who show a total lack of consideration for others. "Some people are fiddling with their bags or fiddling at the tee just when you're ready to swing. Or they'll walk off the tee before you've completed your swing. Some guys don't pay attention and walk in front of you while you're trying to line up your putt."

Adds Rinker, "I don't like guys who can't be still and move around while you're playing your shot. Other guys talk too much. They can't seem to keep a lid on it, especially when I'm coming up to hit my shot."

Disrupting the pace of the play irks Mark McCumber. "There are a few players who are never ready to play their shot," he said. "That's aggravating.

"Here's another thing that's annoying to me: After making his shot, the player will act like no one else is there and he'll just stride off down the fairway. Or else he'll leave the green and head over to the next tee while you are still putting."

Two players—Steve Elkington and Seve Ballesteros—were mentioned as the top two golfers who practice gamesmanship. "When you're playing with them, you're watching to make sure they're not going to pull something," said one golfer.

Adds another pro, "Elkington is always moving around when you're hitting. You're always a little conscious of him because of where he's standing. He'll 'early-walk' you. During your backswing, he'll take a step toward the fairway. I've never said anything to him, but I know other players have—about clearing his throat, ripping off his glove, stuff like that."

Some golfers would be favorites to play with if it weren't for the galleries they attract. The three who attract the largest galleries on tour are John Daly, Fred Couples, and Greg Norman. "The crowd is running all over the place, meanwhile you have this four-footer that's a knee-knocker," says one player.

"Daly's crowds are the worst," says another. "You've got a lot of first-timers, a lot of drunks and rowdies. John has a great rapport with them, and he encourages them. Sometimes I don't think he does enough to control them and get them to be considerate of the rest of us."

After being paired with Daly for two days during a 1993 tournament, Brian Henninger said he felt "like a ghost out there" because the huge crowd only cared about Daly. "Heck, if I was a golf fan, I'd go out and watch John too," said Henninger. "He's fun to watch—unless you're playing with him. In that case, you can't afford to watch because it will completely throw you off what you're trying to do."

Most days on the PGA Tour, the pros play in harmony and good humor. It's natural for golfers on tour to be friends, says Davis Love III. "People see us hanging around as pals and they ask if being such good friends hurts our game," he said. "Well, no, it helps our game. It's better than playing in a tournament with guys who don't want to talk. Then it's miserable out there. It's hard to play for four hours and not talk."

Sometimes it's hard when your playing partner is a close friend. "It's difficult to have a lot of real friends out on the Tour because you're always trying to beat each other," says Payne Stewart.

In the 1993 Memorial, Stewart's good friend Paul Azinger holed out from the greenside bunker on the 18th hole to snatch the victory from him. "Well, at least he was a friend," said Stewart. "It was disappointing to lose that way, but not heartbreaking. If you let every moment like that break your heart out here, you're not going to have a heart to break after a while."

Lanny Wadkins admits there are guys on the Tour who don't like each other. "They think, 'I can't stand this guy and I don't want to play with him.' I try not to do that. I'm not close to a lot of players, but at the same time, I don't want any enemies. If I'm paired with a guy I don't like in the last round of a tournament, I don't want his personality or my feelings toward him getting in the way of my winning a golf tournament."

One golfer says that he often plays better with difficult playing partners. "I decided to let these guys work for me rather than against me," the pro explained. "The worse they are, the better my concentration is."

Brad Bryant says that sometimes the chemistry is just all wrong between two playing partners even though neither one has any ill will toward the other. "For some reason, I annoy Leonard Thompson," admits Bryant. "I like playing with Leonard but he hates playing golf with me. And we're good buddies. It's not like we don't like each other. We go out to dinner and hang out together. He doesn't hold it against me, but he tells me that he just doesn't enjoy playing with me. Obviously, there's something about my demeanor that troubles him on the course. I'm aware of that, so anytime I play with Leonard, I make an extra effort to stay out of his way."

Many players say pairings don't matter because they get along with everyone.

Sibling Rivalry

On the pro circuit, there is one pairing that exchanges words not likely uttered between any other playing partners. That's because the pairing consists of Laurie Rinker-Graham and her brother Larry Rinker.

In 1982, she joined the LPGA and he gained his PGA Tour card. Each December, they compete as a team in the JC Penney Classic at the Innisbrook Hilton Resort in Tarpon Springs, Florida—an event they won in 1985.

"We have a good time playing together," said Rinker. "But we don't take any grief off each other. If one of us chokes on a shot, the other will say, 'What's going on? Let's get it together. Quit fooling around.' Another pairing wouldn't talk to each other that way."

Say What?

What do playing partners talk about during a round? Much the same things that people chat about during their coffee break.

"Primarily, common interests," says Larry Rinker. "A lot of guys are like me—they like music and fishing. A good-looking girl in the gallery always draws a few remarks.

"Then there is talk about golf, of course. Playing conditions are always a topic of conversation. Take, for instance, the wind. I'll tee off on a hole and then say, 'You know, that wind really switched.'"

Donnie Hammond says playing partners usually talk about women, or if both are married, they brag about their kids.

"The guys who are making the big money talk about stocks."

Playing partners tend to find common interests to talk about, says David Peoples. "Things like fishing and hunting. Not a whole lot of talk goes on about golf swings. However, we do talk about golf in general, like the silly little policies of the Tour or about the next stop on the Tour."

"You try to find some common ground with each playing partner," says Bill Murchison. "We talk about clubs and equipment. I played with Lanny Wadkins and we talked about some of his endorsements."

When Mike Hulbert isn't golfing, he's usually fishing or talking about it. "I'm an avid fisherman, so when someone is talking to me, it's usually about the outdoors," he said. "A lot of guys on Tour fish, so that probably is the number-one topic of conversation."

The Fastest and Slowest Players on the Tour

Golf magazine put a stopwatch on the PGA Tour pros throughout the 1993 season to identify the fastest and slowest players on the course. Said *Golf,* "Disregarding walking time, [John] Daly would hit three shots in the time it takes [Nick] Faldo to strike a single putt." Here are the ten fastest and slowest players, in order, on the Tour:

The Rabbits	*The Turtles*
John Daly	Nick Faldo
Hubert Green	Ronnie Black
Don Pohl	Bernhard Langer
John Huston	Ian Baker-Finch
Craig Stadler	Mark Brooks
Lanny Wadkins	Harry Taylor
Lance Ten Broeck	Scott Simpson
Ken Green	Billy Mayfair
Fulton Allem	Greg Norman
Fuzzy Zoeller	Dan Forsman

The Speed Demons . . .

John Daly and Mark Calcavecchia teamed up for a two-hour, three-minute round at the 1992 TPC and shot 80 and 81 respectively. That's not the record, though. The unofficial two-player mark goes to Greg Norman and Mark O'Meara. During the 1988 Nabisco Championships at Pebble Beach, they were way off the lead so they teed off first. They literally ran around the course, playing in a breathless one hour, twenty-four minutes. Both shot 79.

John Huston is one of the fastest golfers on tour. That's because he takes no practice swings in the fairway, in the rough, on the tee, or on the green.

"I never have," said Huston. "That's how I started playing, without taking a practice swing. So I've never thought about doing it."

Before Daly became golf's speed demon, Lanny Wadkins was considered the fastest linksman.

"Want to see a man being tortured?" asked one pro. "Watch Lanny during five-hour rounds at the Las Vegas Invitational. Lanny can play a hole faster than [noted slowpokes] Bernhard Langer or Nick Faldo can line up a putt."

Wadkins says he's never thought of himself as a fast player. "Contrary to popular belief, I don't set any land speed records," he said. "I want to play a comfortable round of golf. I just don't take long to make up my mind. I never have."

Wadkins says he tries to walk slow because otherwise he will catch up to his playing partners and then stand around and wait for them. "I like to walk up, find my yardage, and hit the shot. I actually do stop and smell the roses when I walk."

. . . and the Slowpokes

One of the top complaints among the pros is slow play. It throws everyone's rhythm off.

"If you get out of position with the group in front, perhaps because of a ruling, then you try to play faster to catch up," explained Payne Stewart. "If you try to play fast to catch up and the others in your pairing aren't making that effort, it will screw your game up. I try to tell the guys, 'We are out of position,' because if somebody doesn't say it, the official will be coming over to tell us to speed up. And if he comes over, he's going to start timing us—and that will make everybody skittish."

Adds Donnie Hammond, "The overall pace of play in the majors is really upsetting. The administrators [of each major] only stage one tournament a year. You'd think they'd take a little advice from the rest of the PGA Tour and at least get golfers around in four and a half hours."

Practice rounds are notoriously slow, he complained. "I usually play only nine holes. It's so bad out there that I've got to play at 7 A.M. or 4:15 P.M. to avoid the slow play. It's especially bad in the majors. It goes on forever. Guys are ridiculously slow and they make it tough on everybody."

■

How slow is Nick Faldo as he contemplates a putt?

Says Johnny Miller: "You start your soft-boiled eggs by the time he's ready."

Wagering War

During practice rounds, the pros' most popular gambling game is called "hammer."

"Most of the guys play it out here," said Gary Koch. "Say your original bet is fifty dollars a hole. At any time during a hole, if a player feels he has the advantage, he can call 'hammer.' At that point, his opponent either agrees to double the bet on the hole and play for a hundred dollars or he forfeits the hole and loses fifty dollars. Some major bucks can change hands quickly in that game."

Who are the biggest bettors during a practice round?

Lanny Wadkins
Blaine McCallister
Raymond Floyd
Paul Azinger
Payne Stewart
Mark Calcavecchia
Andy Bean
Fuzzy Zoeller
John Daly

Lanny Wadkins is the top gambler during practice rounds, say his peers.

"Lanny will play for anything, any amount of money you suggest," claims Paul Azinger. "We usually play ten-dollar hammers and ten-dollar one-downs." (Ten dollars is added to the bet if you lost the last hole.)

Wadkins says he bets in practice rounds to help him prepare for the tournament. "I try to play like I was playing the tournament," he explained. "It's important to get a feel for a shot with a little heat on it. It's not so much the amount of money we are playing for. It's the pride.

"I could be playing Azinger for a dollar or a hundred dollars. It's not going to change anything. We are still going to go at each other and have a little fun. It's bragging rights. That's what counts. It hurts him so much to pay me—even a dollar—on the 18th with other people watching."

He said the toughest competitors he's ever played

against for their own money are Raymond Floyd, Arnold Palmer, Bert Yancey, Tom Weiskopf, and Hale Irwin.

Wadkins and Tom Watson often pair up to form a profitable team during practice rounds. "Lanny and I have played a lot of money games together as partners," says Watson. "We had a good game with Freddie Couples and Mark Calcavecchia in 1992 at the British Open. I made a lot more money on the Tuesday practice round than I did missing the cut."

Raymond Floyd would rather play a practice round alone than play one without some money on the line.

But it isn't the chance to win money, he explains. "If money had been my motive for anything, I don't think I'd ever have been worth a flip. I'm not gambling on the golf course. I'm practicing winning. When you're going one-on-one, there's no second, third, or fourth. You have to win."

Nick Price says the most money he ever won in a practice round was five hundred dollars. The big loser? Tom Watson. "I'm not a big gambler," said Price. "But I like to have a little bet going. A hundred a side is enough for me."

During a practice round at the 1994 British Open, Brad Faxon, Davis Love III, Corey Pavin, and Ben Crenshaw each put up one thousand dollars. The golfer who could play eighteen holes without a bogey would win the pot. Faxon played a flawless round and walked off with three grand in his pocket.

Before the Heritage Classic at Harbour Town a few years ago, Bert Yancey and Lanny Wadkins took on Tom Weiskopf and Arnold Palmer for twenty bucks.

"It was our standard game—a team deal with automatic one-downs. Only twenty bucks, nothing outrageous," Wadkins recalled. "It was just competitiveness and the chance to give the other guy the needle. We'd joke and if you missed a putt, you'd get razzed by your partner and the other guys too."

Wadkins and Yancey whipped Palmer and Weiskopf handily, so Palmer told the victors, "We're going to go an emergency nine." Wadkins and Yancey won again.

Recalled Wadkins, "Now, this is Tuesday and we just played twenty-seven holes. It'll be dark in an hour and Palmer says, 'We're going nine more.' We're saying we haven't got time. But he insists because he's not going to lose money.

"We played the last two holes in the dark. And we beat them again. That's thirty-six holes in practice on Tuesday. Can you imagine that happening today?"

When Marco Dawson joined the Tour in 1991, he was quickly hooked into early-week money games by the veterans.

Recalls Dawson: "One day a guy comes up to me and says, 'Wanna play a gammin' game for twenty dollars a hole?' I said, 'Sure, I'll play a gambling game.' And this guy is thinking to himself, 'I've done hooked me a rookie.'

"So on the first hole, we get to the green and he says, 'I'm gammin' you.' I reply, 'Yeah, we're gambling here.' And he says, 'No, I'm gammin' you.' Then he explains that gammin' means doubling the bet on that hole. It took me three holes to realize that by gammin' I was down $120.

"But then I shot about ten under the rest of the way and won $280. And who was this gammin' kind of guy? Andy Bean. Makes the story all that much better, doesn't it?"

You Bet You Were Taken

Mark O'Meara holds an unofficial record for the lowest score ever shot by a pro who still lost money to amateurs.

At home in Orlando, he frequently plays for friendly wagers with amateur pals at Isleworth Country Club, the course where he holds a membership. Sometimes, though, he's too nice for his own pocketbook. Way too nice.

"I'm a soft touch," he admitted. "I get to the first tee and ask the guys, 'How many strokes do you want? Tell me what will make an even game and we'll play.' Most of the time they really take advantage of me."

Such was the case in 1992 when O'Meara played with three good friends. The pro played a near flawless round, shooting a sizzling nine-under 63 on a course designed by Palmer. But when the group totaled the bets, O'Meara had lost fifteen dollars.

"I need someone to explain that to me sometime," O'Meara said. "They had all kinds of different [betting] games going on that I didn't understand. The next time I'm going to know all about them before I tee off. I shoot a 63— and I'm paying those bandits money. I don't get it."

A Snakebit Gambler

Nothing will stop Irish golfer David Feherty from trying to win a friendly wager—not even a snakebite.

During a practice round, which included several side bets, a snake was harmlessly wriggling its way across the 11th tee at Wentworth when Feherty's playing partner Sam Torrance clubbed it with his five-iron.

Recalled Feherty, "I rolled the snake on its stomach and said, 'Sam, it's an adder, the only poisonous snake in Britain. You don't want to touch that.'

"But when I went to flick it away, I hit it flat and the little bugger popped up and caught me right on the end of the finger." The angry and dazed snake then slithered off into the woods.

"Torrance and I were up [about five hundred dollars] at the time, so there was no chance of me going back to the clubhouse. We played on. My finger got bigger and bigger and stiffer and stiffer." But he wasn't about to lose the chance to win the round, which he and Torrance did.

"By the time I got treatment, my finger was quite nasty. I mean, who gets bitten by a snake in England? I spent seventeen winters in South Africa and never saw one. But at least I won the round."

The Pranksters

Pranks for the Memories

**Who are the funniest
pranksters on the Tour?**

Paul Azinger
Payne Stewart
Gary McCord
Peter Jacobsen
Phil Blackmar
Willie Wood
Billy Ray Brown
Lee Trevino

The biggest prankster on the Tour is a toss-up between Payne Stewart and Paul Azinger, according to the players.

"Payne is number one," says Donnie Hammond. "He has these crazy teeth that he slips on and tells everyone he got in a fight with somebody the night before and got his mouth all busted up. They look so real it's unbelievable. He has several gags like that."

Azinger is at the top of Mark McCumber's list of zany jokesters.

"One time I was on a plane to Milwaukee and every once in a while, I would feel drops of water on me," McCumber said. "During the flight, I noticed that the flight attendant was walking down the aisle and water was dripping off her hair. I was looking around for the source and I called her over. We all thought the water was coming from a vent.

"When we landed, I was getting off the plane when I noticed that my pants were wet in the front. I thought, 'Gosh, I don't think I wet myself.'

"I looked over and there was Zinger a few seats away and he was just dying laughing. All this time he had a small squirt gun and he was secretly shooting everybody on the plane—flight attendants, businessmen, and fellow pro golfers. The gun was about the size of his hand, so nobody could really see it."

McCumber claims that Azinger even shot the squirt gun during the Greater Milwaukee Open. "That whole week he went around and shot people in the gallery. He would walk off the green and nail them. And the funniest part was that they didn't even know what was happening. They would look up, like, 'It's not going to rain, is it?'

"The tournament officials finally asked him to stop squirting people. Paul's a harmless practical joker. We need more guys like him and Payne Stewart. The majority of golfers on the Tour are too serious."

Stewart and Azinger have inspired others to pull practical jokes in the otherwise conservative world of golf.

Once when Tour player Gary McCord was acting as a CBS color man on a golf telecast, he told the audience that Willie Wood was a great prankster. "The problem was that Gary did some serious exaggerating," Wood recalled. "He said that I had super-glued Phil Mickelson's shoe trees to his shoes. That wasn't true."

So Wood decided to get even with McCord. "The next

day, I super-glued all the zippers on Gary's bag. Later, he came up to me and said, 'Okay, I won't mention the shoe trees trick anymore.'

"Billy Ray Brown likes to pull a practical joke every now and then. So a couple of us guys decided to get him one time during a Sunday night football game between the Dallas Cowboys and the Philadelphia Eagles. We were all in a skybox enjoying the game which was being televised by ESPN.

"We arranged for someone to come up to the skybox and tell Billy Ray that [announcer] Joe Thiesmann wanted to interview him live on the air. Billy Ray said sure and went down and stood by the ESPN trailer for about fifteen minutes, waiting for someone to come out and get him for the interview. Then he saw all of us off to the side laughing, and he knew he had been tricked. He's still congratulating us on that one."

Wood said that baby powder figures in several common practical jokes on the Tour. "It's pretty harmless, but a small amount can make a big mess, especially if you put it in the bottom of a guy's golf bag," he said.

"A real good joke is to put some baby powder in a hair dryer. When the guy gets out of the shower and his hair is still wet and he turns on the blower, baby powder sticks to his hair and skin. He has to go take another shower. That's a good one."

Bill Murchison said that one of the best jokesters on the Tour is an official, Wade Cagle. "He's always pulling tricks. One of his favorites is putting a fake snake in front of golfers. That gets them hopping."

Gene Sauers says John Huston likes to joke around the clubhouse. "If a player gets a big picture in the paper during tournament week, Huston often will clip it out, draw a funny face on it, and pin it up in the locker room."

The Payne and Paul Show

Payne Stewart and Paul Azinger are close friends, fierce competitors, and great pranksters. They especially like pulling jokes on each other.

"We're both very competitive and we thoroughly enjoy giving each other a very difficult time when it comes to needling," said Stewart.

It was Stewart who taught Azinger that there is no disappointment so great that it can't be the foundation for a little joke.

The ultimate example came at the 1993 Memorial when Azinger beat Stewart with a dramatic hole-out from a bunker on the 18th. It was an emotionally devastating loss for Stewart, who had led most of the day. In his victory speech, Azinger spoke of his sorrow for his close pal, who, Azinger presumed, was back in the locker room that very moment choking back tears.

"Here I am, kind of left holding the bag," Stewart recalled. "All of a sudden, I figure, 'Well, I'll get even with him.' So I was sitting in the locker room by his locker. His tennis shoes were right there.

"Now, these are some pretty old tennis shoes for somebody of his stature and abilities to be wearing. So I decided, 'Well, I'll fix him.' I just took a banana out and broke it up and stuffed it in the toes of each shoe."

Said Azinger later, "I knew he was okay when I got back to the locker room and there were bananas stuffed up in the toes of my shoes."

But now it was payback time.

While playing a practice round at the Tour Championship at the Olympic Club in San Francisco in 1993, Stewart was victimized by Azinger. Each time Stewart reached the tee, he discovered the water cooler was empty—and in each case there was a message scrawled on the side.

"On every cooler was some mean message complaining

there wasn't any water in it," Stewart recalled. "They would say 'Bone dry.' 'Where's the water?' 'I'm dying of thirst.' And every single one had my name signed to it. It couldn't have been anyone else but Zinger. He's just got a devious mind. He's a kid at heart, but a kid with a devious mind."

Another time, while Stewart was giving an interview at the media tent, in walked Azinger wearing a pair of Stewart's trademark knickers. "He had coerced my wife into giving him a pair and he interrupted my press conference by trying to mimic me," said Stewart. "Obviously, he wants to be like me."

■

Once, friends of both golfers targeted Stewart for a practical joke. "At Christmastime, I was sitting around playing cards with some of our buddies, including an NBA referee," recalled Stewart. "The ref had brought everyone a gift. They opened up their boxes and got an NBA T-shirt.

"Now, I love NBA T-shirts. So I open up my box, expecting to get one, but instead there's this baggie of sand. It comes with a note that says the sand is from the exact spot where Paul had holed his winning shot on the 18th at the Memorial. They got me. They got me big time."

■

Stewart and Azinger teamed up to nail their mutual friend Lee Janzen after he won the 1993 U.S. Open.

In honor of his victory, they sneaked into Janzen's locker and left bananas in his regular shoes. Recalled Azinger, "We asked him later if he found the bananas and he said, 'I can't believe you guys put bananas in my shoes. Didn't you see my note?' I said, 'What note?' It turns out he left a note on top of his shoes that said, 'No bananas, please.' It must have fallen down between the shoes.

"But how's that for confidence? He wrote that note before he went out Sunday morning and won it. That's awesome, man."

These Greens Were Tough to Read

In a long-standing Masters tradition, the reigning champion gets to set the menu for the Champions Dinner the following year.

Ben Crenshaw, the 1984 winner, decided to spice up the fare in 1985. He arranged for a big tray of appetizers that included hot jalapeño chiles disguised as pickles.

"Well, both Jack Nicklaus and [Masters chairman] Hord Hardin were digging in, and all of a sudden they both grabbed for a big glass of water," Crenshaw recalled. "I looked over at Hord later and he had sweat all over his forehead. But he never said anything."

How Do You Say 'You Got Me' in Spanish?

During a tournament in Mexico City, Lee Trevino was on his way to dinner with twenty friends at a fancy restaurant. Riding with him was his good friend Pete Zagganino, a Connecticut lawyer.

Trevino told his pal it was a Mexican custom to express great appreciation to the waiter after the meal was finished. Zagganino, who knew no Spanish, asked Trevino what he should say.

"Just grab the waiter and say, 'La cuenta, por favor.' And don't worry. I'll let you know when to say it."

After a long and festive meal of drinks, appetizers, more drinks, entrees, more drinks, desserts, and still more drinks, Trevino nudged Zagganino and whispered, "Now, Pete, now."

Zagganino grabbed the waiter and said cheerfully, "La cuenta, por favor."

He had no idea that he had just asked the waiter for the bill. As requested, the waiter handed the unsuspecting American a tab for $1,200—while Trevino and his friends bolted with laughter from the table.

Temper Tantrums

Teed Off

Some of the nicest guys on tour have the hottest tempers and often flare up at their own mistakes.

"It's no secret that Steve Pate has a massive temper," said one pro. "He's called the Human Volcano because that's what he is. When he erupts, it's fierce. It can be pretty embarrassing at times for him and all those around him who see it. But it's part of his persona, and it works for his game."

Pate says he had to learn to control his fiery temper in order to improve his game. He admits his nickname was well deserved.

When things went awry on the course, Pate said, "my anger would build slowly and then it would come to a boil. I would yell and then it would be over. Then I would tell myself, 'That was pretty stupid.'

"When I was younger, I would spend six or seven hours being ticked off. That didn't help my game much.

"I've been that way since the first day I picked up a golf club. But I only get mad on the course and always at myself."

His most embarrassing explosion occurred at the 1991 Kapalua Invitational. Pate was in contention when he hit a wayward drive. As he bent down to pick up his tee, he snarled loudly to himself that the fairway was "nine . . . miles wide." He used a vivid adjective that many consider terribly obscene.

Unfortunately, Pate had erupted within earshot of one of NBC's directional microphones and he was heard by a national TV audience. The PGA fined Pate for the outburst. Meanwhile, NBC's golf announcers called Pate "Volcano" so often that one of the companies Pate endorses talked to him about his temper. They said it wasn't the image they wanted Pate to project. He, in turn, asked NBC to cool it on the nickname, which the announcers did.

In an interview with *Golf* magazine, Pate's teaching pro, Jim Petralia, recalled Pate's early, tempestuous days. Petralia said all he had to do to beat Pate on the course was get him mad. Recalled Petralia, "He threw clubs. Stomped around. Hit himself. He would take his putter and beat his foot to death. One time he was about to break a club. I told him, 'Give me that. I'll break it for you.' That *really* got him mad.

"In one respect, his temper is what makes Steve as good as he is. He can't stand to lose."

What players have the hottest temper?

Steve Pate
Hale Irwin
Mark Calcavecchia
Jose Maria Olazabal
Dudley Hart
Carl Cooper
Simon Hobday

Carl Cooper has been known to blow up at himself. "One of the worst tempers may be Carl," said a pro. "At one tournament he broke a club over his knee, put the two broken pieces together and snapped them over his knees—and bloodied up his hands in the process."

Several players claim Dudley Hart can erupt in a flash.

"You'd never think it," said Willie Wood. "He's so nice and friendly off the course. Then you put him on the course and he shows a terrible temper. I remember one time on the 7th hole at Westchester, he almost got into a fight. Dudley was getting angry over his play and then a spectator started mouthing off. Dudley started mouthing back and the next thing you know, they were setting up a place to meet after the round."

Hart says that ever since he joined the PGA Tour in 1992, he's had to battle not only his fellow competitors but his temper as well.

"I can be hard on myself and I get upset sometimes," Hart admitted. "I've always been a perfectionist. I focus on the one bad hole instead of the seventeen good ones. But I've gradually learned to deal with it."

He has worked with Virginia-based sports psychologist Bob Rotella to keep his temper in check.

"I've gone the other direction where I pretend not to care, but that's just not me," said Hart. "Then I feel like I'm going through the motions. It's a fine line for me. I've worked on using my temper to my advantage. When you hit a terrible shot, you can mope around and say, 'I can't believe I'm playing bad' or you can slam a club and say, 'I'm going to get up and down from here.' Ninety percent of the time, I'm like that.

"I've beat myself up pretty good in the past. But now I'm trying to be my own best friend. I'm kinder to myself. I'm learning more about the game and myself every year."

Even golfers who aren't considered hotheads still have occasional blowups.

Says Irish golfer David Feherty, "I can get pissed off as much as the next guy. I broke my toe once by taking an enormous kick at my bag. It was very satisfying until the point of contact.

"And the other day, I nearly gave myself a brain hemorrhage. I wanted to scream at the top of my voice, but I screamed inside myself."

John Cook said he used to verbally abuse himself on the course. But then, while he was home recovering from a hand injury, he was watching golf on television and noticed that temper tantrums were crippling some of the players. "I got myself to reflect on more positives than negatives now."

Nick Faldo says he's been working on taming his temper, but he still maintains it's not good to bottle up your feelings.

"I used to be far more disgusted with myself when I blew a shot," he said. "I was hard on myself. Some days you can handle things well and some days you can't. If a shot means a lot and you screw it up, you're bound to call yourself names.

"Some of the players on the course do it right—they get it out of their system right then and there. If you hit a bad shot, you can't just say, 'Oh, well, I just bogeyed the hole' and continue on your merry way without feeling something inside. You've get to let it out or you'll make yourself sick."

However, he said, he appreciates Fred Couples's attitude. "Freddie has this great attitude. Once he's hit a shot, it's gone. If it's bad, so what? There's nothing he can do about it. I think that's great."

Senior PGA Tour player Simon Hobday would win more tournaments if he could just tame his temper, say his peers.

"He's a great guy and a superb golfer," said one player. "But that temper gets in his way."

Added another player, "If he hits a bad shot, he gets angry at himself when he should be staying cool and planning his next shot."

Hobday is the first to admit that he owns a quick temper. "I get pissed off," he admits. "I simply don't understand how someone can hit a ball that lands in the water and say, 'Well, that's golf.'"

During the 1994 PGA Seniors Championship in Palm Beach Gardens, Florida, Hobday plunked two balls into the drink on a par-3 hole. As he stormed toward the pond, he snarled, "Two balls in the water. By God, I've got a good mind to jump in and make it four!

"I tell you, a man has to be thick as two planks to play this game."

Later, he complained to a gathering of fellow bar patrons, "Golf giveth and golf taketh away. But it taketh away a hell of a lot more than it giveth."

Lost Cause

During the Chrysler Great 18, a made-for-TV golf event in 1993, John Daly lost his temper—and his clubs.

On the 18th tee at Pebble Beach, Daly told playing partner Fuzzy Zoeller, "If I hook this ball in the water, I'm going to throw this damn driver in."

"You don't want to do something crazy like that," said Zoeller. "You've had enough trouble this year."

Sure enough, Long John hooked his drive into the Pacific Ocean. Seeing how fuming mad Daly was, Zoeller held out his hand and asked, "May I?"

Daly handed him the club. Zoeller then tossed Daly's driver fifty yards out into the water.

Moments later, Daly botched several more shots along the way to the hole, and pitched two more clubs—his two-iron and eight-iron—into the surf. When he finally finished the hole, the disgusted Daly gave his golf bag and the remaining clubs to a little girl in the gallery.

Curtis Strange on winning back-to-back
U.S. Open titles in 1988 and 1989—the
first to do so since Ben Hogan
accomplished that feat in 1950 and 1951:
"In 1988, when I won my first Open,
I had to pinch myself once in a while.
Then to do something nobody else had done
in a long time, in 38 years, that was
something else. I thought, 'Why me?'
But then I thought, 'Why not me?'"

Bryant's Strange Conversation

For many years, Brad Bryant had a reputation as a hot-tempered complainer. But he's changed.

"I used to have a real bad problem with constantly complaining on the golf course," he admitted. "A lot of guys didn't like to play with me because all I did was complain and get mad at myself. Playing partners don't need to hear me complain."

Bryant said he eventually worked hard on improving his demeanor on the course and toning down his anger when he made a bad shot. But then he learned something from Curtis Strange—who often struggled to keep his fury in check—when the two were playing together at a tournament in 1993. According to Bryant, the conversation went like this:

Strange: "You shouldn't get mad at yourself so much."

Bryant: "I don't understand what you're saying because I feel I've made a great change and don't complain like I used to."

Strange: "No, that's not what I'm talking about. You need to get mad. But you get mad at the wrong time."

Bryant: "I don't understand."

Strange: "If you hit a bad iron shot, you get mad. But you shouldn't get mad because of a bad shot."

Bryant: "Now hold on. Why shouldn't I?"

Strange: "Well, if you hit a bad iron shot, you still have three ways to make par. You can hit a good chip; or make a good putt; or hit a mediocre chip *and* a mediocre putt and still make par. If you're going to get mad at yourself, do it for making a bad score. Getting mad over a bad shot can cause you to make a bogey when your goal is to make par. If you don't make par, then kick yourself in the butt. But give yourself the very best chance you can to make pars."

In recalling the conversation, Bryant said that he's seen Strange hit a bad shot but remain amiable. "Until he told me his secret, I never really understand how he could stay so calm. Now I know. Bad shots don't matter to Curtis. Bad scores do.

"That talk, coupled with the change in my driving, has had an enormous influence on the way I play."

Craig Stadler was asked why he was using a new putter at the 1993 U.S. Open. Replied the Walrus, "The old one didn't float too well."

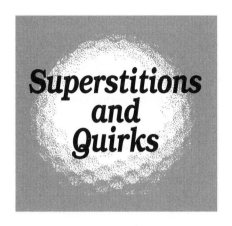

Superstitions and Quirks

Luck of the Links

Many players have their quirks when it comes to courting good luck.

Larry Rinker won't play with a high-numbered ball. "I mean, it's not a real positive thought process when you look down at your ball and see the number seven on it. You don't want to be thinking 'seven' when you're standing on the tee."

John Cook carries two lucky coins as markers—a dime and a nickel. "But they must have good years on them," he added. To Cook, good years include 1975 when he got married, 1979 when he turned pro, and 1992 when he enjoyed his biggest money-earning year ever.

Among other lucky charms used as markers are:

• Hale Irwin's Japanese coin with a hole in the middle;

• Jay Haas's British coin;

• Charles Coody's British halfpenny that his daughter gave him.

When asked about his own superstitions, Gary Koch said, "I prefer to call it a routine. I carry the same number of tees in my pocket every round and I hit the same number of wedge shots to warm up for each round." He didn't say what those numbers were.

Some players use balls numbered one or three because thirteen is their lucky number. Others have food superstitions. "If I play particularly well, I will eat the same breakfast that I had for the next few days," said one pro who didn't want to be named because "I don't want people to know I'm superstitious."

Many players believe that the right color of clothes can have a positive effect on one's performance.

Seve Ballesteros always wears blue for the final round. Senior PGA player Larry Mowry says he dons red clothes to give him confidence.

"If I play a particularly good round, I'll remember the outfit I wore and will wear it again real soon," said Larry Rinker. "Once in 1993, I shot a course record 63 in a pro-am wearing this black and gray outfit. A couple of weeks later, during the first round of a tournament, I was playing so-so and was two over par after six holes. Suddenly, I realized that I had on that same black and gray outfit. I said to myself, 'Hey, this outfit can get hot. Let's bear down.' I played the last twelve holes in eight under par. What an outfit! By the way, I have some dog-playing outfits too that I don't wear very often."

Coody has this thing about the color red. "He's the most superstitious player I've ever seen," says Koch. "On the PGA Tour, he always wore red socks when he thought he needed an under-par round on Friday to make the cut. It didn't make any difference what color shirt or pants he wore. If Charles had on red socks, you knew he needed red numbers on the scoreboard."

Don't Tees Me Like That

Golfers are very particular about the color of their tees and refuse to play with certain colors. For instance:

• Bob Tway won't play with red tees because red is one of the colors of the University of Oklahoma—archrival to his alma mater, Oklahoma State.

• Blaine McCallister won't use orange tees because orange is one of the colors of the University of Texas—a school that the former University of Houston grad loathes.

• Jeff Sluman won't be caught dead with blue tees.

Chi Chi the Charmer

Chi Chi Rodriguez is a charming man—in every way imaginable.

Not only is he personable, but he's also superstitious and relies on several lucky charms to help him on his rounds. "I'm very superstitious," Chi Chi admitted. "I think everyone is a little bit, but they don't want to admit it."

Among the lucky items he carries in his pocket are:

• A tiny marble stone that was blessed by the pope and given to him by a fan;

• A lucky walnut;

• A quarter to mark his ball on birdie putts;

• A buffalo nickel to mark his ball on par and eagle putts;

• A gold piece when the quarter or nickel isn't working as a good-luck marker.

"I won't use a ball with a number higher than four because you can't make a four with a five," Rodriguez says. "I will never mark my ball with a coin that is tails. In fact, I won't even pick up a coin if the tails is showing.

"If I have a good round, I like to drive to the course the same way the next day. And I like to wear green on Sunday because green is the color of money."

Despite Rodriguez's reputation as the king of superstition, he says he doesn't get too carried away in his beliefs. "One time in 1987, a guy in Jamaica put a voodoo doll in my bed," he recalled. "The doll had a nail through each eye and knee. The guy thought that I believed in it and would play badly. Well, it didn't work. I had a great year."

That Old Jack Magic

On the morning of the opening round of the 1994 U.S. Open, Jack Nicklaus was putting in his contact lenses in the bathroom of his hotel room when his wife Barbara cast a spell on him.

"I'm going to hypnotize you," she said, raising her arms and wiggling her fingers for effect. "It's 1962 and you're twenty-two again."

The fifty-four-year-old star looked at his wife, wondered for a moment how he should respond, and then did what most husbands do. "I accepted what she said," he recalled.

Barbara's spell seemed to work magic. Nicklaus played like the same golfer he was back in 1962 when he won the Open in a playoff over Arnold Palmer. In the first round of the 1994 tournament, he drained a forty-foot birdie putt on the 18th hole and walked off with a sterling two-under 69.

Unfortunately, the spell vanished after the first day and he finished in a tie for twenty-eighth.

"I always feel like a twenty-two-year-old," Nicklaus said. "I just don't always play like one."

Mind Games

What do you think about when you're standing over a pressure shot?

Fred Couples: "Actually, I think of a good shot that I have hit in the past—whether it was years ago or yesterday.

"One thing you don't ever do is think of bad things when you're over the ball. People might think about bad shots, but I don't—even on shots I might be scared to hit.

"I will visualize shots like the six-iron I hit [at the 1992 Nissan Los Angeles Open] against Davis Love III on the 14th hole in the playoff at Riviera. It won the tournament for me. When I'm on the 18th at Augusta, I think of Riviera. I say to myself, 'I'm here at Riviera' and picture the ball fading. Every shot I do that, whether it's a pitching wedge or a two-iron.

"I never think of the bad shot I just made or bad things in the past when I'm standing over the ball. But sometimes as I'm walking to the ball, I'll mumble things like, 'I can't believe you just did that' or 'I can't beat anybody.' I try to catch myself and get rid of those kinds of thoughts by the time I reach my ball."

Lee Janzen: "Before a shot, I just make sure that I take my time lining up my shot and telling myself to trust my swing."

Tom Watson: "When I am playing my best, I'm not thinking of very many things. Just whatever the shot requires.

"Usually I have one solid thought. It's often a feel or a rhythm on the takeaway and that is all I worry about; not on the way down or the follow-through, just the beginning of the swing. Put it in motion and it will happen."

Nick Faldo: "I have always believed in golf that you cannot mentally make something happen if you physically haven't got it. You can't say, 'I am going to hit this two-iron with a fade and stay right of the pin.' Then a little voice says, 'Hang on, have you got the swing for that one, mate?'

"Then you are not going to do it. But once you have the confidence, once your swing and everything have given your mind the confidence, then it is all mental. Your mind will automatically tell you, 'Do this. Do that.'

"I have swing keys. They are really good for you under pressure. Other guys under pressure might think, 'Oh, my God, what am I doing here?' But I can stand up and say to myself, 'All right, it's forward, slow, out, rotate.' It's the same routine again and again. That's the way I do it and that takes away the pressure because I know exactly what I'm trying to do. I know my swing keys and just get up and produce it."

Tom Kite: "I think good thoughts about golf most of the time," he said. "It's a choice you have. You can either choose to think good thoughts or bad thoughts. A lot of guys have a lot of talent. But they don't do as well as they should because they're not thinking as well as they should."

Raymond Floyd: "First, let me tell you what I don't do. I don't try to pep-talk my way into a good shot by saying, 'You can do it.' That's self-delusion. Nor do I minimize the importance of the shot. There are Tour pros who tell themselves, 'It's not that big a deal—either you pull off the shot or you don't.' I say, if that's your attitude, you're not much of a competitor.

"I confront the fear head-on and try to work out a physical solution to the mental problem. During my practice rounds, I try to develop a shot that will enable me to step up to the tee with a positive attitude and make a confident swing."

Corey Pavin: "I talk to myself to maintain my confidence. Instead of putting pressure on myself and thinking, 'I've got to make this shot,' I think, 'Go ahead and make it.' It's a subtle difference, but a big one."

Nick Price: "Sometimes I feel something in my swing that reminds me of what I used to do badly. It happens at such unusual times and it hinders me. I try to find ways to put those bad thoughts and feelings away or use them to strengthen my resolve not to make those same mistakes again."

Brad Bryant: "I practice visualization. The clearer you can visualize the shot, the greater chance your body has of producing it. If you don't have a real clear picture before you hit, the shot will come up fuzzy. That's the reason some of the great players are pretty slow. When they get under pressure, they take a whole lot longer to visualize the shot. They aren't relying on their mechanics at all. In fact, they throw their mechanics out the window.

"That's the way Jack Nicklaus is. He can see the height, the trajectory, everything about the shot. He spends some time before swinging the club because it takes him a while to visualize the shot clearly in his mind.

"Watch Nick Faldo. He stands there forever. Finally, he pulls the trigger and he hits a wonderful shot. That's because he saw the ball flying toward the hole before he ever hit it."

Phil Blackmar: "When I get into a pressure situation—when I really need to make a good swing or a solid stroke—

I try to visualize something positive. I think good thoughts. I don't really try to relax. If I'm relaxed, that means I'm not really focused. I have to be at least a little nervous to do well."

What do you think about between shots?

On the course, players don't think about golf every second. Sometimes they get lost in a daydream or let their mind wander just like the rest of us.

So, what *does* go through their heads as they're walking down the fairway?

Ian Baker-Finch: "I like to take in the scenery. I'll stop and watch a hawk circle above me."

Larry Rinker: "I just pray a lot when I'm out there."

David Peoples: "I think about the kids, dinner, and other sporting events. As a University of Florida grad, I think about how the Gators are doing."

Bill Murchison: "I sing a lot, mostly songs that I have written. I also sing scripture songs. I keep my mind on spiritual things as well as on the family and trees and birds."

Fuzzy Zoeller: "My mind wanders all the time. Some days I think about everything and then there are other days when I am really focused on my golf."

Mark McCumber: "I think about my wife Paddy and my three kids. Sometimes my mind drifts to things about my [golf course design] business. Some guys might be able to stay in a mental bubble for four hours, but most of us can't. I usually think about the outdoors or something peaceful."

Mike Hulbert: "I look at the lakes and imagine what kind of fish are in there. I also look at nature and see the beauty of the golf course."

Winning Thoughts

Golfers think of the strangest things when they are about to win a tournament.

In 1991, Fulton Allem was 143rd on the money list. If he didn't finish third or better at the Independent Insurance Agent Open in Houston, he would lose his playing card. The South African had resigned himself to the bitter reality that he might soon be playing back in Europe.

At the start of the final round, he was seven shots off the lead and four shots out of third place. Teeing off early, he fired a 66.

So what was he thinking when he drained his last putt and had to wait for the rest of the field to finish?

"I didn't think I'd win, even when I walked off the 18th green at fifteen-under," he admitted. "I looked up at the leader board and there were guys out there at fourteen-under and they had eight holes left to play.

"The only thing I said to myself was, 'Don't let three guys beat me or I'm going to lose my Tour card.' That's all I wanted. I wasn't thinking of winning the tournament. I just wanted to keep my Tour card. Winning never entered my mind. I was sitting there thinking the only way anybody could prevent me from keeping my card is if three of them make a two on the last hole. As I'm thinking that, Tom Kite's ball was in the air. Then it hit the flag. I went cold."

But Allem needn't have worried. None of the three contenders behind him caught up to him. Allem won his first Tour event and pocketed $144,000—and kept his Tour card.

Two years later, when he blitzed through the final round of the NEC World Series in an eight-under-par 62 to win by five strokes, he wasn't thinking about the $360,000 first-place check. All he kept thinking about was the coveted ten-year exemption to PGA Tour events that goes to the World Series champion.

"I can't describe the feeling," he said. "To have a ten-year exemption is worth winning ten tournaments to me. It means that much."

■

It took Paul Azinger eleven years on the Tour to win his first major when he captured the 1993 PGA Championship.

As he walked off the green, having defeated Greg Norman on the second playoff hole, "it brought tears to my eyes," Azinger said.

"I thought, 'What a huge burden off my shoulders.' I knew I was good enough to win a major championship. I always claimed I never had to prove anything but to myself. I knew people were talking about me being the best player not to have won a major. I think that put a lot of added pressure on me. So as I walked off the green, I kept thinking, 'Now it's over . . . and I'm glad.'"

■

While on the 18th hole, ready to claim the green jacket for winning the 1992 Masters, Fred Couples had to wait for playing partner Craig Parry, who was searching for a lost ball.

Going through Couples's mind were not thoughts about the Masters. Instead, he turned to his caddie, Joe LaCava, and said, "Can you believe the Knicks only scored 37 points in the first half against Detroit?"

■

When Lee Janzen won the 1993 U.S. Open, he embraced his wife Beverly on the 18th green at Baltusrol and hugged her tight. "I just thought about how much I loved her," he recalled. "There was nothing else like it. To have a wife like I have, to be able to share that moment with her."

■

In the final round of the 1990 B.C. Open, front-runner Nolan Henke refused to look at the leader board until the turn. His mind wasn't on trying to win the tournament, only to finish eighth or better so he could keep his Tour card for the following year.

Recalled Henke, "I glanced up at the leader board on the 15th hole and thought, 'All right, I'm safe. Don't make a double or triple [bogey] or do something real stupid.'

"I birdied the 16th and I looked up at the board again just to make sure my name was still there. I told myself, 'I've got a four-shot lead with two holes to go. I should finish in the top eight.'

"On the 17th hole, I started to get nervous and thought, 'If I don't win this, all my friends at home are going to laugh me right into the ground.'

"By the 18th, it was 'I have to win it. I can't just finish in the top eight.'" Henke parred the last two holes and walked off with his first Tour victory.

■

When Fuzzy Zoeller won the 1979 Masters in his fifth year on the Tour, he immediately thought back to when he was a youngster, dreaming about this moment.

"I had a putt on the 11th green [to win in a playoff] and my mind was reverting back to when I was growing up," Zoeller recalled. "I would stand over a putt back then and pretend it was for the Masters. I was hoping then that one day my dream would come true. Mine did. It's wild what your mind does."

To this day, says Zoeller, he can recall every shot he made at the 1979 Masters.

"I remember my first practice round at Augusta. I played with Hale Irwin. He looked at me and said, 'Kid, just look around.' He showed me a couple of plaques [of great golfers]. And I just kind of got into it. Winning there is a feeling that's hard to put into words what it does to a person."

Mr. Positive

How positive is Chip Beck?

Listen to what some of his fellow pros say.

Raymond Floyd: "Chip could find a way to find something positive about the *Titanic* going down."

Paul Azinger: "If Chip learned an earthquake had destroyed a major city, he'd be the first to point out that half the city was still standing."

Gary McCord: "If a car ran over and killed Chip's dog, he'd marvel at how peaceful the poor beast looked."

Norman Vincent Who?

Nolan Henke never met Norman Vincent Peale or read his best-selling book *The Power of Positive Thinking*.

That's because to Henke, nothing could be more negative for him on the course than to think positively. He plays golf with a mind-set thrown in reverse.

Henke displayed his negative psyche at the 1991 U.S. Open when he was one shot out of the lead after two rounds. A reporter asked him, "Do you think you can win the tournament?" Henke replied, "I know I can't win. Well, I guess I could—if everyone else broke their leg."

Henke has perfected the art of negative thinking to work to his advantage. He's won three tournaments in his first five years on the Tour and finished thirty-first on the 1993 money list with $502,375.

"I don't go out there with the idea that I'm going to play really well," he said. "I do that because if I know I'm playing really well, I'll try too hard and end up not playing well."

To Henke's way of thinking, if you expect little of yourself, then you're seldom disappointed. It doesn't work for most people, but it works for him. "If I end up with a good score, that's great," he said. "If you set your goal at breaking 80, then every time you go out, you're probably going to have a good day." Most every day is a good day for Henke, because he virtually never shoots an 80.

According to his longtime coach, Mike Calbot, there's nothing wrong with this unorthodox approach. "All Nolan is doing is taking pressure off himself," said Calbot. "He pushes himself to excel as hard as anybody in the game, but what's different is that he doesn't set himself up for failure before he ever begins to play."

Say a Little Prayer

When Corey Pavin stands over a difficult, pressure-packed putt, he prays.

"It's not like, 'Please let me birdie this hole,'" he said. "It's nothing like that. It's just been, 'Lord, let Your will be done. And, whatever You have in store for me today, let it be done.'

"It's been more of an acceptance of what He has in mind for me. As long as I do the best I can and try the hardest I can, then it's His will that will be done for me."

Pavin believes that prayer has helped make him even more competitive because it allows him to use his God-given abilities to the maximum.

Prayer also relaxes him. "Sometimes when you want something so badly you get anxious and uptight about it. Previously, I'd want something so badly that when I played poorly, I'd step on myself. I'd get in the way of myself. I'd get so uptight and so nervous and so worried that I'd perform at a lesser level than my capacity." He said when he feels himself slipping mentally, he begins to pray and becomes more relaxed without losing his intensity.

"I said a nice prayer before I hit my last putt at the Ryder Cup [in 1993]. I bent down to line up a two-footer to win the match. Adrenaline was flowing at the most rapid rate I've ever felt. I was bowing my head for about five or ten seconds. I said a prayer to let His will be done, to let me relax and hit the putt the best I can. I got over the putt and made it."

Confidence Games

Every golfer wants to win—but few really believe they can, says Brad Faxon.

"There are a lot of tournaments that Tour players go to— and this will surprise the hell out of people—and they don't try to win," Faxon claims.

"You're not ever going to win if you don't have the confidence to do it. It doesn't 'just happen.' You've got to believe you can win before it's going to happen."

Faxon worked on his confidence level in steps, taking one small victory and building on that for the next.

"One of the things I wanted to do at the start of 1992 was to be near the lead as many times as I could," he said. "That's great preparation. It helps you when you finally get into the lead. It makes you comfortable, playing in those situations.

"For most people, getting close to the lead changes what they do. I wanted to get enough experience just being there that I would be relaxed enough to play my game."

The approach seemed to work for Faxon. He won two of his four tournament victories in 1992 when he finished eighth on the money list.

Faxon was perhaps the best player in the world for one month during that year when he won the New England Classic and the International and lost a playoff at the Buick Open.

He credits his success to being totally focused.

"I really focused mentally on just being ready to play,

and to actually think about winning," he said. "When I teed it up for the first hole, I thought about winning. I didn't think about just making a good paycheck."

There are times, admits Greg Norman, when he, like most every other golfer, plays in "so-so land"—when he begins to lose confidence and second-guesses himself.

"That's when you confuse yourself," he said. "You think, 'Why am I doing this? How do I stop it? Is my club in the right position at the top? Is my rhythm out? It's 183 yards. Is it a little four-iron or a hard five-iron?' You start getting all these things going through your head, all these conflicting thoughts and feelings.

"You start thinking, 'Is the wind blowing four miles an hour from the left?' You get too much going into the equation, and the golf swing is such a simple but complex move, you can't have a lot in the equation because it happens so fast."

He found himself in "so-so land" at the 1991 Western Open. "I was working on something in my swing and I lost my train of thought," he recalled. "Now all of a sudden, I'm losing ground. I'm three-putting and I'm starting to get uneasy. Now I'm thinking, 'God, the front nine I played so great. What's happening here?' I lost the feel of what I was doing. That's because I was trying to be too mechanical instead of being basic and natural."

Sometimes too much confidence is just as harmful as too little, warns Nick Price. "I learned my lesson at the 1982 British Open," he says.

Back then, Price was a twenty-five-year-old pro standing on the 13th tee in the final round at Royal Troon. He had just birdied the last three holes to take a three-stroke lead.

Price turned to his caddie and boldly said, "Well, we've got it now."

Price then was tripped up by his own overconfidence.

"I bogeyed the 13th, double-bogeyed the 15th, and finished with a 73—one stroke behind Tom Watson," Price recalled.

"Immediately afterward, I was really depressed. At that stage in my life, twenty-five years old, I played well enough to win a major championship. I don't think there are too many people that age who've come that close.

"But then I worked my way out of the depression. I told myself that I had fifteen to twenty years of my career ahead of me. If I worked on the right things and analyzed my mistakes and tried to correct them, then I figured I'd be a much better golfer. So that's what I set out to do."

By 1993, he was the leading money winner on the Tour with nearly $1.5 million in earnings.

"Maybe it helped me not to win the British Open in 1982. Maybe if I'd won it, I would've thought, 'Hey, I've got all the game I need.' Maybe that experience was a blessing—although I don't know if losing the British Open is ever a blessing."

■

Early in the 1993 season, Lee Janzen wrote in a spiral notebook all the things he had to do to concentrate better on the course. He also listed his goals for the year—one of which was finishing in the top ten of a major.

When Janzen captured the 1993 U.S. Open, a reporter asked him why he had set his goal so low. Janzen replied, "I can't dream this big."

"If I ever think anybody is better than me, then I can never be the best. I always have to believe I'm the best."

—Payne Stewart

Focus Groups

The best players focus only on their next shot and block everything else out of their mind. Few are as focused as Raymond Floyd.

"Raymond is a no-nonsense player," says Mike Hulbert. "He goes into that zone and just freezes everything else out of his mind. He concentrates solely on his golfing and won't allow for distractions."

Who are the most focused players on the Tour?

Raymond Floyd
Nick Faldo
Corey Pavin
Bob Estes
Jeff Maggert
Bernhard Langer
Curtis Strange
Tom Kite
Jack Nicklaus

Floyd is one of the greatest competitors on the Tour because he's so focused, claims Payne Stewart. "It's his internal makeup. He has such a tremendous desire to compete that he has managed to stay completely focused. He has his outside business interests, but he hasn't let them interfere with his ability to play such a high level of golf. On the course, his eyes seem to be staring at something you can't see."

Says Brad Faxon, "Raymond is ready to play Thursday morning at the first tee every time. Some guys don't get into it until the sixth hole. If some of us could be as focused as Raymond 50 percent of the time, we'd be great players."

Floyd "grinds as hard as he can whether he's shooting a 78 or a 68," says Mark McCumber. "That doesn't mean he's not friendly. He's just focused."

McCumber says that Corey Pavin is unbelievably focused. "He's an absolute fireplug. I was covering his round on NBC at the Ryder Cup when he was playing against Peter Baker. Baker did not miss a putt. He made five or six thirty-footers and many eight-footers. Corey didn't even flinch. It was unbelievable. I think that Corey is, without question, the fiercest competitor on the Tour."

Like Pavin, Lanny Wadkins says that he's so focused he sees nothing but the ball and the hole. "To me, the gallery becomes nothing but a wall. I don't even see faces."

Nick Price says he admires the focus displayed by Jack Nicklaus. "He's so totally focused on each shot that if you ask him, 'What's going to happen on this hole, Jack?' he wouldn't be able to tell you because he's only thinking about the one shot that he's faced with at that moment."

Nicklaus says he tries not to get stirred up by the crowd. "I have never fed off the gallery's response, especially early in a tournament," he said. "I think the galleries are terrific, but I am trying to figure out how to hit a golf shot. I am never really bothered with the outskirts. My concentration is on what I am doing.

"Probably the only place that I fed off of the gallery a little bit was coming down the stretch at Baltusrol in 1980 [where he won the U.S. Open]. That was almost dangerous going from the greens to the tees [because of the crush of fans], and it was wild, but obviously, I couldn't avoid that. But I try to keep myself fairly level if I can. If I get too excited, I have a hard time playing."

It took Chip Beck several years to discover the true meaning of focus. "I used to stand over an important putt and think about all the money at stake," he said. "But then I learned to relax, like the great ones, and think only about the ball and the hole."

Payne Stewart said Lee Janzen won the 1993 U.S. Open over him by two strokes because Janzen remained focused. "The thing I like about Lee is his emotion," said Stewart. "He's not easily rattled. That's the best way for a golfer to be. Don't get involved in other things around you."

The Zone

When a player is performing at his optimum and the shots are falling exactly where he wants them, then he's in "the zone."

Explains Nick Price, "The zone is the ability to give 110 percent of your attention and your focus to the shot. When I'm on the tee, I'll see a divot in the fairway and try to run my ball over that divot—and succeed. That's the zone."

Price says he was in the zone during the 1993 Players Championship, which he won with a remarkable eighteen-under-par 270. Price, who beat runner-up Bernhard Langer by five strokes, hit 61 of 72 greens in regulation.

"That was four days of flawless ballstriking," recalled Price. "It was as if I was standing outside myself and watching me make those shots. To me, that was the ultimate, to make the game look so easy from tee to green."

Greg Norman was in the zone during the 1990 Doral-Ryder Open when he blistered the course with a 62.

"In the zone, you get so focused, you don't even know what score you're shooting," he said. "When I holed that third shot on the 8th hole, I knew I was going to hole it. I *saw* it going into the hole [before hitting it]. So I hit it as fast as I could because I didn't want to lose the feeling. Boom. It goes in.

"You have to be careful not to get carried away with the things that are happening outside the zone. People are jumping around and screaming. You know what's going on outside there, but you don't want to let it in.

"You just have that ability to make your golf club part of your body. You don't feel your golf swing. You don't get confused by any thoughts. You don't see water out there. You don't see the bunker six or eight feet in front of the pin. I can put a ball within a foot or two feet of where I'm aiming from 183 yards. It's one of those things that you just can't explain."

Raymond Floyd says that when he gets into a zone, he is hardly aware of anything but the next shot.

"I get a sense of total focus, total involvement in what I'm doing. I don't hear anything. I've looked straight at my wife in the gallery and not seen her. It's a perfect zone—the mental and physical are sort of fused. There's a lightness in my step and yet I feel as if everything is moving at half speed.

"I'm not hitting the ground very hard when I walk. I'm aware there are people around, but I don't see them. I might talk to the player I'm walking with, but I don't know it. I'm alone and I'm at ease."

Floyd's Focus

Never was Raymond Floyd more focused than he was at the 1992 Doral-Ryder Open. Less than three weeks earlier, fire had destroyed his 12,000-square-foot Miami home. Almost everything he owned went up in smoke.

"My golf trophies, believe it or not, meant the least," he said. "They meant nothing, really. It's the little things with absolutely no monetary value, the irreplaceable little pieces of life that really matter.

"What mattered were all the photographs of dear close friends, parties, happenings, ball games, fishing trips, our wedding, the children, the whole family album, the entire history of us. It was the worst thing that has ever happened to me."

Fortunately, no one was hurt. Raymond was in San Diego when he received the call from his wife Maria at 1:08 A.M. "I'll never forget the time on the clock," he said.

When Floyd came home, he sorted through the rubble, cried, and then picked a new architect to rebuild on the same spot. Finally, Maria told him that she would deal with the contractors and insurance people if he would get ready for the tournament. "She said she'd take care of everything else if I would take care of the family by going out and playing," Floyd recalled.

The Doral-Ryder Open was being held only a few miles away from the site of his burned-out house. As he walked on the course, well-wishers offered their condolences. But he didn't totally hear them. He was in the zone.

"I had this tremendous urge to respond on behalf of my family," he said. "There was a need. I just had to perform. I honestly think I was inspired. 'Damn it,' I told myself, 'this family needs some good news. We've got to get this fire behind us.'"

Even though he hadn't won a PGA Tour event in six years, the incredibly-focused Floyd burned up the "Blue Monster" with a blistering seventeen under par to capture the tourney's title.

"I count that a team title," he told reporters afterward. "The Floyd team won at Doral," he added, pointing to his beaming family—Maria, teenage sons Raymond Jr. and Robert, and teenage daughter Christina.

Pavin the Way to Victory

When it comes to focusing, Corey Pavin is one of the best on the Tour. He credits part of his success to his "brain coach," Dr. Richard Coop, a University of North Carolina professor who counsels athletes.

During the 1992 Honda Classic at Weston Hills in Fort Lauderdale, Pavin was locked in a playoff with Fred Couples. As Pavin was about to hit his tee shot, some rowdies in the gallery shouted, "Shank it! Hit it in the water!"

While such heckling might break the concentration of many pro golfers, Pavin looked at the hecklers and laughed. He stepped away from the ball, still grinning, and wiped his grip. Then he got back in position, drew back his driver, and nailed his shot perfectly down the tunnel that he had visualized for himself. Moments later, he beat Couples by sinking a fifteen-foot birdie putt.

Afterward, everyone was talking about the eight-iron Pavin had holed on the 18th to get into the playoff and the birdie putt that won the tourney. But for Dr. Coop, the biggest factor in Pavin's win was how the golfer handled the hecklers. "I appreciated that much more than I did the crucial shots he made," said Dr. Coop.

During practice sessions, Dr. Coop has deliberately tried to disrupt Pavin's concentration by heckling him. But Pavin has learned how to remain focused.

"When my students study the difficulties of staying focused in critical situations, I can't think of a better example than Corey's at the Honda Classic," said Dr. Coop.

Pavin has never lost a head-to-head playoff since he joined the Tour in 1984. He's beaten Seve Ballesteros,

Craig Stadler, Steve Pate, Fred Couples, and Dave Barr in playoffs.

"It seems like when he has a putt that really means something, Corey rises to the occasion and drains it," said Barr. "If you're on the green with him and you have to putt first, there's a lot of pressure because you know he's probably going to make his."

It wasn't always that way. Pavin's temper often jarred him enough to lose his focus. Several times, after bad tee shots, he smashed his driver against the tee markers so hard it exploded like a bomb.

But then he worked with a golf instructor on a new swing and developed an improved mental approach with the help of Dr. Coop. The next year, 1991, Pavin soared to the top of the money list.

But despite two tournament victories and earnings of nearly $980,000, Pavin said he was most proud of his worst round of the year. At the 1991 U.S. Open at Hazeltine, Pavin began the third round one shot out of the lead. But he blew up to a seven-over-par 79 and eventually finished eighth.

"In a way, that was the highlight of the year," he said. "I went out and just played lousy the whole day. My game was gone. But the thing I did well that day was I just kept trying. I kept my faith up that things were going to get better. I just kept at it and at it. I never got upset at anything during the day. I kept playing one shot at a time and tried really hard on every shot.

"When I finished the round, I knew I had done the best I could—that day. And that was an important thing for me. Sometimes your best is 79. It was a round that probably a few years ago could have destroyed the rest of my year. But it didn't even faze me. I went out the next day with the same attitude and shot 72 and finished in the top ten anyway.

"In other years, I would have been out there saying,

'What's wrong?' But I proved to myself the next day, by swinging exactly the same way, that there was nothing wrong. It was just golf. Some days you go out there and the ball just doesn't do what you want it to do."

■

In 1991 Ian Baker-Finch had a series of sessions with sports psychologist Bob Rotella, who overhauled the golfer's mental approach to the game.

"The biggest thing he did for me—the key to my success—was to get me to try to hole every shot, to try to focus wholly on knocking every shot into the cup from the fairway," recalled Baker-Finch. "I stopped thinking about getting up and down, knocking it on the green and one-putting. I started thinking about holing the shot at hand. And even though that sounds unrealistic, it really helped me focus. That was the biggest stumbling block I had to overcome."

Three months after his initial sessions with Rotella, Baker-Finch won his first major—the British Open.

The Picture Perfect Shot

"When you stand behind the ball and picture the perfect shot, and then you get up there and pull it off, there is no feeling like it in the world," claims Curtis Strange. "It still feels the same to me as it did twenty years ago. And as long as that feeling is there, I'll be there. I guess the allure of golf is really the next shot . . . always trying to hit it perfectly, to get that feeling.

"The mystery of golf is that nobody can master it. You can shoot a good score today, but can you do it tomorrow? Why does it leave you? Why does it come back? Why can one guy perform under pressure and another can't? How much can you ask from yourself and how much can you give? That's what I get into, that's what I think is neat. If you have the guts to reach down far enough, it's almost inhuman some of the things you can do."

A Well-Trained Pro

Arnold Palmer likes to tell this story about Raymond Floyd's psychological approach to putting:

"Once Raymond hit a long putt into the hole and his playing partner says, 'Man, that was great. How did you do that?' And Raymond says, 'I saw a pair of railroad tracks going toward the hole and there was a locomotive going down the tracks. Didn't you smell the smoke?'"

Embarrassing Shots

The Flub Club

Every pro remembers a shot he'd like to forget. Jay Haas said his worst shot in a tournament happened in Europe in 1983. "Thank goodness it wasn't on national television in the United States," he declared.

He made the classic boner of weekend duffers. "I cold-topped it off the tee," he recalled. "It went about a hundred yards, and the only reason it went that far was because I hit it off an elevated tee and the ball rolled down the hill.

"It was really embarrassing. Here I am standing with my driver in my hand and the ball is rolling only a few yards from the tee."

Fulton Allem was playing in Memphis in 1981 when he suffered his most embarrassing shot. It happened on the tee of the par-3 14th hole. "I made a big swing with a one-iron and took an enormous chunk out of the sod. I bumped the ball about twenty-five feet off the tee. The gallery just stood there stunned. My playing partner, Mark Lye, looked at me for a moment, then said, 'Did you catch that one solid?' We both broke up laughing. I had to use a three-iron for my second shot—on a par 3."

Allem's second worst shot occurred at the 1994 Masters, on the 16th hole in the first round. "I folded the sod over the ball, I hit it so fat," Allem recalled. "I actually had to get yardage for my second shot. My caddie had to have been embarrassed as he walked it off. I had 101 yards left from a 170-yard shot. That's not bad—it was only at the Masters, in front of about five thousand people who thought they were there to see the greatest players in the world."

Scott Hoch's worst golfing moment was a series of whiffs in front of a live television audience in a tournament in Hawaii. "I was eight under after thirteen holes," he recalled. "Coverage had just come on TV and they zeroed in on me immediately. Just as they did, I hit a ball onto the roots of a tree. I got down and took a few practice swings without hitting the roots. Then I wound up for my real swing and I bounced the club off the roots. I didn't even touch the ball.

"I stepped back and said, 'Well, I'll try it again.' I stepped up, hit the roots, and bounced the club over the ball again!

"I finally just tapped the ball a few inches until I could get it away from the roots. It took me a couple of more taps before I could get the ball out to where I had a full swing at it."

When Hoch was on the golf team at Wake Forest University, he discovered how fickle the game is during a college tournament—all because of a sweater.

"It was really cold in the morning, but then it warmed up," he recalled. "I took off my sweater, which was kind of a confining sweater, as I walked to the 10th tee. Coach Jesse Haddock was there plus a lot of other people. And then I topped my tee shot. Not a pure top, but real thin, one that carried maybe a hundred yards.

"I was playing pretty good at the time. But then I topped my tee shot again on the next hole. In fact, the whole back nine went like that—just one missed shot after another.

"At the end of the round, Coach told me, 'Don't ever,

ever, ever take your sweater off in the middle of a round—
especially if it is the least bit restrictive. When you take it
off, all of a sudden you have a lot more freedom and your
swing changes. It is the worst thing you can do. Go ahead
and sweat if you have to, but don't go changing anything
once you start playing.'

"To this day, I don't take off a sweater unless the heat
just gets unbearable."

Gary Player confessed that in the most mortifying shot of
his illustrious career, he was knocked out by his own ball!

It happened during a tournament in Leeds, England, in
1955. "I had come to England for the first time and I had
only 250 pounds in my pocket and I wanted to stay there
for six months, so I really needed the money," said Player.

"I was playing the final hole, a par 4. I thought I needed
only a five to win the tournament. Why the hell I took a
driver off the fairway I don't know. It was this crappy old
yellow-looking wood with a funny shaft. I hooked my ball
against an old English stone wall.

"So now I thought, 'I've somehow got to get this ball up
on the green so I can make five.' I concocted a plan to try
to ricochet the ball off the wall and bounce it up there.

I took a big cut and . . . pow! . . . the ball bounced off the
wall and came back and hit me right in the head. It
knocked me out. Flat knocked me out. I took boxing in
school several years earlier and I never got knocked out.
But I did get knocked out there on the course.

"They put smelling salts under my nose. I was really
groggy, but I managed to get up and hit the ball onto the
green in four. When I went to putt, I was seeing two cups,
but I knocked the ball into one of them. I was so happy. I
was jumping up and down with my five and saying, 'I won!
I won!'

"A guy walked up to me and said, 'Gary, you've got a
seven.'

"I said, 'No, I've got a five! Count them up.'

"He replied, 'You've got a seven. You hit yourself, that's a two-stroke penalty.' That was a first-place prize of three hundred pounds that I didn't get. At that time of my life, three hundred pounds was like bloody gold."

Mark O'Meara said he hit a shot so bad that even his competitors felt embarrassed for him.

"It was at Cherry Hills in the U.S. Open," he recalled. "On the 18th tee in the second round, I pulled out my driver and I hit the ball about sixty feet—right into the water.

"I looked at the two guys who were playing with me to see if they were going to laugh. They were both looking away. I guess they were so embarrassed for me that they weren't going to say a word.

"For about five seconds, I thought I was just going to quit golf because I didn't think anybody had ever hit a shot that bad. Those are the times when you look down and stare at your club—as if, for some reason, it was your club's fault instead of your own pathetic swing."

Dan Pohl has a reputation for being one of the longer hitters on tour, but he hit an unforgettably short shot one time with his driver. "It was on the first hole of the 1983 PGA Championship at Riviera Country Club," he recalled. "I was paired with Jack Nicklaus, so obviously there was an enormous crowd.

"That hole has a high, elevated tee overlooking the fairway. The wind was blowing left to right, and since I hit a 'cut' ball, I had to actually aim toward the out-of-bounds area to keep it in the fairway.

"So here was this enormous mob of people behind me, and I take a three-wood, trying for control and accuracy. I dropped the ball on the ground and took a big swing—and I thumped the ground behind the ball.

"Thank goodness I was up on the hill. The ball rolled about forty yards down to the bottom. I just tucked my head down and wanted to slip away."

Paul Azinger said he suffered his most inglorious golfing

moment during his rookie year on tour. "It was at Pensacola and I was playing a practice round with Mark Calcavecchia and Ken Green," he recalled. "At that time, I always used a two-wood off the tee.

"Well, on one hole, I cold-topped the ball and it rolled fifty yards. So I laughed and said, 'I better take a mulligan.' Then I cold-topped the second one. You know what everyone around me must have been thinking? 'Man, what a hacker.'"

Wayne Grady still winces when he recalls his worst shot. "It was in Japan, at Chunichi Crowns," he said. "I was playing with Jumbo Ozaki, the most famous golfer in Japan, with about ten thousand people following us. On a par-5, I had a five-iron shot left to the green.

"I hit a cold shank. I nearly hit the hole-in-one car—on another hole! My ball was fifty yards short and fifty yards right of the green. You couldn't dream of a more pathetic shot. And it had to happen in front of everybody in Japan."

Blaine McCallister said his most inglorious moment occurred during the 1988 Los Angeles Open. A huge gallery had gathered around the 18th green to watch his second shot.

"I was thinking, 'I can hole this shot,'" McCallister recalled. "I swung and then looked up to see where the ball was going to land. Everything had the sensation and the look that I had hit the shot.

"But when I looked down, the ball was sitting in the divot. The club had gone completely under it. I kind of tipped my hat a little lower over my face and wanted to cover the name on my bag. You just know those people were saying, 'He's a what? A pro?'"

Fuzzy Zoeller winces when he recalls the time he tried to hook a four-iron around a tree at New Orleans. "I took a bunch of practice swings, just like it says to do on page 35 of your instruction book," he said with tongue in cheek. "And then I gouged a huge divot that simply flopped over the ball. It was like someone had placed a hairpiece over it."

Mike Reid suffered his worst brain sprain ever during a tournament at the Showboat Country Club in Las Vegas. "Two times I hit approach shots from the fairway—an eight-iron on one hole and a four-iron on the other," he said. "My caddie had the perfect yardage. And both times the shots were right at the pin. The only problem was, I was aiming at the wrong pins! They were on different holes. I've never done that before or since."

Hale Irwin's moment of misfortune occurred not at some insignificant event but at the British Open, in 1983. Tied for the lead in the third round, his eighteen-foot birdie putt on the 14th hole hung on the lip. When Irwin went to backhand the ball, his putter caught the ground and missed the ball. He lost by a stroke to Tom Watson.

"It was the most bizarre thing that's happened to me," said Irwin. "I was in absolute shock. You play this game long enough, and you'll do it all. And you can't laugh at anything anyone else does—because either you've done it, or you're going to do it."

Splash Down

Raymond Floyd has the reputation for being one of golf's greatest front-runners. True to form, he had a four-stroke lead at the turn of the final round of the 1994 PGA Seniors Championship.

But then, in a matter of a few shocking minutes, he plunked two balls into the water on the 15th for a quadruple bogey and one ball into the drink at the 17th for a double bogey. The mishits led to an eight-shot swing and handed the title to Lee Trevino.

"I was as shocked as he was," said Trevino. "He gave it to me on a silver platter. Raymond was Santa Claus."

Said Floyd, "I've been around this game long enough to know it can leave you just as quickly as it comes to you."

As his caddie walked from the scoring tent beside the last hole, a youngster asked for a ball to keep as a souvenir.

"We left them all in the water," the caddie said with a cynical smile. "We've got none left."

Gary McCord, the quip-witted golf
announcer for CBS and sometimes Tour player,
says this about his so-so golfing career:
"I started off very slow and then I tapered off."

Wacky Shots That Worked

Golf, even for the pros, is not all style and grace. Sometimes the best shot is one that only a duffmeister could fully appreciate.

During one Masters in which he was struggling, Lee Trevino decided to have some fun. "There had been so much rain at Augusta that the lake in front of the 16th was as high as the bank," Trevino recalled. "I took my one-iron and told the official, 'Watch this.' I hit the ball on the water and it skipped across and up on the green. I two-putted for par from about thirty feet and felt better about my week."

Johnny Miller needed to play the last four holes under par in order to make the cut in a tournament in England. "I hit a drive through the fairway and into a clump of trees and found my ball stopped by a big tree trunk," he recalled. "I took an old Tommy Armour putter and hit the ball left-handed through a three-foot opening in the trees ten yards away. My ball flew out about 160 yards and hit seven feet past the cup, and backed up five feet. I holed my putt for a birdie and made the cut. It wasn't what you'd call your high-percentage shot."

During another English tourney, Bernhard Langer lofted a ball that lodged in a tree branch about fifteen feet above the ground. "I decided I had a good shot if I could reach my ball, so I rolled up my trousers, climbed the tree, and balanced myself on the branch," he recalled. "Sure enough, I hit the ball to the green and sank my putt for a par." What club did he use? "A tree iron," he cracked. (For the record, he used a pitching wedge.)

At the 1992 PGA Championship,
a reporter asked Jim Gallagher Jr.
this dumb question:
"What's your father's first name?"

The Intimidators

Scare Tactics

Raymond Floyd is an intimidator. He has that stare that seems to bore through his opponents like a laser. Yet, he pretends he doesn't know what everyone is talking about.

"I've never felt that I was mean on the golf course," he says. "I know that people say that I intimidate people with my looks and stuff. But I'm not aware of that."

Says 1992 Player of the Year Fred Couples, "There aren't many guys who intimidate me. But he does."

Adds Mark O'Meara, "I told Raymond he's the most intimidating player I've ever played against. He plays every

---

Who are the most intimidating players on the Tour?

Raymond Floyd
Fred Couples
Nick Faldo
Curtis Strange

---

shot like it's the last shot of his life. He's like a black leopard, stalking the jungle."

Lanny Wadkins declares that he's not in awe of anyone on the Tour. "Not Nicklaus, not Palmer, not Watson. Never have been. I've beaten these guys in tournaments down through the years and I'm not going to be intimidated. I refuse to be."

He believes that Fred Couples can intimidate younger golfers without saying a word.

"He makes it look so easy," says Wadkins. "He's not very talkative. Some people mistake his quietness for complacency. I think he's trying his damndest to win. You don't win what he's won and not have a lot of drive and competitiveness. He's got plenty there."

Curtis Strange and Nick Faldo are "by far the most intense guys out there," and can intimidate the younger golfers, according to Brad Bryant.

"I love playing with Curtis because of that intensity. I feel like every time I play with him, I learn something about staying focused. He may go around and hit only two good

---

Who are the most aggressive players on the Tour?

Lanny Wadkins
Fred Couples
Ken Green
Davis Love III
Tom Kite

---

golf shots all day, yet he'll still find a way to beat you because of his intensity."

Lanny Wadkins brought his attack-the-course reputation with him from Wake Forest when he joined the Tour in

1972. Put the flagstick in the parking lot and he'll try to find a way to hit it with a three-wood.

"It's just kind of my nature to go for it," said Wadkins. "That's what makes it fun. I've always felt it was so tough to win on the PGA Tour that you have to keep going for it and hope you get hot. That's when you win."

Ken Green says that if he has a choice, he'll always take a chance on pulling off a great shot.

"Ask yourself this question," he once said in *Golf Digest*. "Why do you play golf? Is it to plod around, never attempting anything not well within your capabilities? Or is it to live on the edge, trying to pull off career shots you'll reminisce about years from now?

"I don't know about you, but I like to have fun while I'm playing golf, and fun for me means attacking the course."

Green says he made himself an aggressive player when he was growing up by fining himself if he didn't reach certain lofty goals that he had set. "If I didn't accomplish what I set out to do, I would leave a five-dollar bill in the cup or on the range. When you're young and poor, losing five dollars hurts a lot."

Tom Kite is considered by his peers as one of the gutsiest players on the Tour. Says Peter Jacobsen: "Tom has the least amount of ability, but he leads the Tour in guts and the ability to get the ball in the hole."

■

Nick Faldo says his attitude is: "If you need a par, go for a birdie, because if you don't get the birdie, you should hopefully get the par. It's the same thing if you go for the best.

"If your goal is to go out and win $100,000 a year so you can pay the mortgage and feed the wife and the kids, then that is what you will do. You'll never win a major or become the best.

"If you are money oriented, try and win a million dollars

in a year. Because even if you fail to win a million dollars, you are sure going to pass $100,000 pretty quickly."

■

During the 1993 Masters, Chip Beck was roundly criticized when he elected to lay up with his ball 236 yards from the front of the 15th hole. He was in second place at the time, trailing Bernhard Langer by three strokes in the final round.

When Beck took his hand off the cover of his wood and reached for his five-iron, CBS-TV announcer Ken Venturi told his viewers that Beck was "protecting second."

Meanwhile, back in Orlando, Arnold Palmer, who was watching the action on TV at his home after missing the cut, went ballistic. He screamed at the TV, "Go for it!"

But Beck played it safe, parred the hole, and finished in second place. "I was hitting that shot thinking, 'Man, I hate to lay up here,'" he explained later. "But one thing you have to learn. In any situation, you have to be your own person. You have to play your style and your game. You have to be true to that, no matter what the outcome."

Beck's critics pointed out that in 1935, Gene Sarazen was faced with an almost identical situation. He took out his wood and hit the golf shot heard 'round the world— making a double eagle 2 that helped give him the Masters victory.

> Two reasons why Chi Chi Rodriguez likes to play aggressive golf:
> • "I was born broke, I'm going to die broke, so I might as well go for broke."
> • "I never play conservatively. I only dress that way."

Why do the pros say Corey Pavin is the toughest competitor on the Tour?

Mark O'Meara: "He's like a little dog that gets hold of your pants leg and won't let go."

Gary McCord: "He's got a really nice pit bull mentality."

Paul Azinger: "Intestinal fortitude. Corey has more of it than anyone else. Just plain old intestinal fortitude."

Billy Andrade: "He's tough as nails."

Steve Pate: "Corey isn't satisfied unless he's beating the hell out of everybody all the time."

Jay Delsing: "He loves to compete. He's not particularly strong, but he's totally unafraid."

Lanny Wadkins: "He's a battler. He doesn't back off an inch. He's the worst kind of guy to face. You look at guys like him—different kind of swing, small in size—and you think you should be able to handle him pretty easily. You can't help but think that way, even if consciously you know it's wrong."

Mark McCumber: "There are some pretty tough guys on the Tour. But no one is any tougher than Corey. He's as competitive a guy as I have ever seen."

■

Although Corey Pavin is arguably one of the most competitive players on tour, he says his emotions aren't that much different whether he wins or loses a tournament.

He credits his faith and philosophy on life with feeling that way.

"After losing, I've felt nearly the same as when I've won," Pavin said. "It's not quite the same, but I haven't been down about losing a tournament. I've been disappointed, but I haven't been discouraged. And when I've won a tournament, I don't feel as elated because it's not as important to me as it used to be, and that's probably why it's easier for me to win."

How to Win a Major

Most of the pros say that to win a major, you have to play consistent, steady golf and let the other guys make the mistakes.

That's how Nick Price won the 1992 PGA Championship. He made ten straight pars to start his final round and didn't try to force anything. And he wouldn't let anything distract him.

"I knew the way the course [at Bellerive] was set up, that if I played smart, I was going to have a chance to be there in the end," said Price. "You have to get to the stage where you say, 'This is the golf course that I have to play this week. The fairways may be like concrete and the greens like mud, but that's the way it is.' The more guys who keep complaining about it, the fewer I have to beat.

"I just remember Jack Nicklaus saying he won more majors when other guys faltered than when he went out and actually won. A good example of that is Nick Faldo. He plays really good golf under the gun and when the other people make mistakes, he's right there to win."

Nick Faldo says he studies the opponent for any flaws.

"I do it all the time, especially in match play," he said. "You're not picking on the guy. You're doing it to build yourself up.

"The first time I played Seve Ballesteros in the World Match Play, I looked at his swing and thought, 'There's no way this guy's swing is going to last thirty-six holes. He's going to make mistakes somewhere.' I told myself, 'Be patient. Sit and wait for him. Don't get all tensed up.' And sure enough it worked."

■

Paul Azinger learned the hard way to never think too far ahead on the course.

At the 1987 British Open, Azinger finished with back-to-back bogies to lose to Nick Faldo. "On the 17th tee, I was already thinking about the presentation ceremony," he recalled. "What I should have been thinking about, of course, was my drive."

■

Lee Janzen says winning a Tour title can play havoc with your mind in subsequent tournaments.

After he won his first championship, the 1992 Northern Telecom Open in Tucson, he tumbled into a short-term slump.

"My game went into shock," he admitted. "I lost focus and got sloppy. I found myself daydreaming during play, thinking back to Tucson."

■

"I started winning in 1986 and it becomes a habit," says Fulton Allem. "It's never easy to win. You handle yourself a little better the second, third, and fourth time you've won.

"I believe in the three D's—dedication, discipline, and determination. In my case, determination is the big thing. You have to really want it more than anything else in the world. It's one thing, believing in yourself. But it's something else to go out and do it."

■

Davis Love III says he constantly has to keep himself from trying too hard.

"I expect to win whenever I play, but I have to be careful of putting too much pressure on myself," he said. "When I'm going good, if I'm doing the right things mentally, then I have the physical ability to just keep making birdies and I can run off way in front. But I can't force that to happen."

He has worked with sports psychologist Bob Rotella for several years. Rotella taught the golfer how to put the last shot behind him and focus on the next shot.

"It's very easy for me to try too hard," said Love. "Bob has taught me that it's sometimes good not to try too hard because you might get uptight.

"You play your best golf by just reacting to the target. If you are focused on the target, you aren't thinking about anything bad happening."

Calling It Quits

A lot of players withdraw for dishonest reasons, claims John Daly, who was suspended for four months after deliberately picking up his ball at the 1993 Kapalua Invitational.

"A lot of guys say, 'My wrist is hurt' when it's not," said Daly. "I'm just not the type of guy who is going to do that. I'm going to say, 'Look, I'm playing bad, I really don't have a chance to make the cut, I'm leaving.'

"I don't see anything wrong with that. If a guy wants to get out of there Friday night to get home and spend some time with his family, then why shouldn't he? But I'm not going to be withdrawing from any tournaments any time soon."

Have you ever just gone through the motions at a tournament?

John Cook: "Probably somewhere I have, but I haven't in the last five years. Before that, I'm sure at some point in time I was at a place I didn't want to be, and it [his golf game] wasn't working. I never want to do that again."

Dan Forsman: "I hate to say it, but I have. I've done it a lot in my career, unfortunately. Sometimes the game just wears you down, and at times it is really tough to maintain such a high level of commitment."

Scott Hoch: "At times I have, but never from the beginning of a tournament or a round, no matter how poorly I may be playing. But once it's inevitable that you're going to miss the cut, then it [going through the motions] can happen. Usually, it's something like not taking as much time over every shot."

Ken Green: "Yes, I have. After I've reached a certain point, when I know I'm done."

David Frost: "I find it very hard to give up, whether I'm going to miss the cut or am lying thirtieth. I find it very hard to say the hell with it and just play. I never give up hope."

Mike Reid: "Granted, some weeks motivation is harder to find. But one of the things I'm proudest of is that in eighteen years, except for injury or health reasons, I've never walked in or given up."

> *"Each time we play,*
> *we leave a little piece of ourselves*
> *on the course. You never*
> *know how much longer you'll be*
> *competitive."*
>
> — four-time winner Dan Forsman

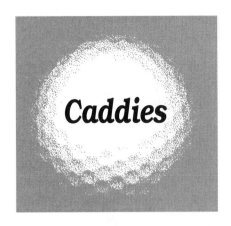

Caddies

Totin' Them Bags

Caddies do more than haul forty pounds of golf equipment around the course. They act as part-time sports psychologists, map course yardages, and help line up putts.

"There are three rules for a caddie to live by: Show up. Keep up. Shut up," says Paul Jungman, who has carried bags for seven years on the Tour.

"It's a slow death, basically, but you've got to die somewhere so it may as well be out here. At least it's exciting. You never know when your week will roll around—when your player wins or when he gets rid of you. If you keep the same player for a year or two, you're lucky. It's like being married. He eventually gets tired of looking at you every morning and vice versa."

Each player uses a caddie differently to fit his particular needs, says Jim Medziak, who often caddies for Roger Maltbie. "One time I was urging a ball to stay up and the golfer told me, 'Hey, I don't want a cheerleader out here. You're not wearing a skirt, are you? Don't talk to my ball anymore.' Other golfers need the conversation from the caddie to break the tension. Some even want you to kick them in the ass to get them going if they need it."

Lee Janzen says his caddie, Dave Musgrove, has been a big influence on his play. "He would slow me down and get me to focus more on hitting shots that I need, not just on the range, but also on the course," said the golfer. "Sometimes when I'm playing, he'd see I wasn't focused as much and say, 'Okay, let's concentrate on the target, aim for the pin.' He's very good."

Ian Baker-Finch credits part of his success to his former caddie Pete Bender, whose aggressive personality is opposite that of the mild-mannered golfer's.

"Ian needed to get a little tougher," said Bender. "I think I helped a little. In my twenty years out here, I've had a lot of experience winning, knowing what it takes to win. I put the whip on him and he listens to me."

For example, in the first tournament the two worked together, the 1989 Kemper Open, Bender immediately let Baker-Finch know who was in charge of the golf clubs.

"Ian had this little chip shot," Bender recalled. "He had hit a couple of bad chips with his sand wedge, and he wanted to hit the pitching wedge for this one, even though the shot clearly called for a sand wedge. He said, 'I'm going to hit the [pitching] wedge.'

"I said, 'Bullshit. Hit the club the shot calls for. Get mean, get confident, visualize the ball going in. Get mean.'

"He said, 'Okay, okay.' He took the sand wedge and hit a chip shot that spun around the cup. I said, 'That's what I want.' He said, 'Thanks, I needed that.' Then he went on to shoot 66 the next morning."

What really frustrates caddies is the tendency of some golfers to blame them for the pros' own shortcomings. "The guys beat us up for things that aren't really our responsibility," said a caddie. "There are golfers who cuss you out on the course and then come up to you afterward and say, 'Hey, I don't remember a thing I said to you today. But if I did say some mean things, I'm sorry.' There are other golfers who look for someone else to blame—and usually it's the caddie."

Says Brian Sullivan, who carries for Jeff Maggert, "With some guys, you hand them a club and they lay sod over the ball with it and then give you hell for the rest of the day. They don't have the wife or kids or dog to kick, so you get it."

There's a saying on the Tour: "Change equipment, then change caddies, then change the swing." As a result, most every caddie has been fired at one time or another.

"It's like managing a baseball team, " says Medziak. "Sometimes a change is needed. The player and caddie can't get along, so the caddie goes. But other times, without any communication, the caddie is gone. I know a case recently where a guy won a tournament with his regular caddie and then fired him two weeks later. Why? The golfer said the caddie was too serious. The caddie asked, 'Was I too serious two weeks ago?' "

Caddie Russ Craver, who split from Larry Nelson for eight years before they got back together, complained to a reporter, "You can work for a guy for years and all of a sudden, one day he says, 'Oh, I don't think we're getting along. Maybe we should split up for a while.' "

No matter how good a caddie is, he usually gets fired or has a mutual parting of the ways with the pro. It's happened to the best of them. Andy Martinez, who used to work for Johnny Miller, once caddied for Hal Sutton. But at the 1987 Masters, he gave Sutton a bad club. The golfer's approach shot sailed over the green and Sutton made a double bogey. He fired Martinez a few weeks later.

"It's a lot of pressure when something you say could cost a player a hundred thousand bucks," said Martinez.

Pete Bender was Greg Norman's caddie in the mid-1980s and seemingly doing fine. Then one day, Norman called him and said, "It's time to change." According to Bender, Norman never gave him a reason.

"Greg intimidates caddies," Bender told *Golf* magazine.

"You're afraid to say stuff to him, even if you're right, because you don't want to be fired for it. I'm not afraid to be fired."

The golfers who caddies say are the good guys to work for:

Paul Azinger
Chip Beck
Jay Haas
Jim Gallagher

The Golfers Caddies Don't Want to Work For

Of all the golfers on the Tour, Tom Purtzer is the one most caddies don't want to work for.

Although most caddies declined to name names for fear of losing jobs, several toters complained about Purtzer.

"He's one of those guys who can't make a decision on his own," claimed caddie Jim Medziak. "Every shot is, 'What club do I use?' 'How hard do I hit it?' 'Exactly how far does this break?' 'Should I wear a hat or a visor?' 'What color sweater should I wear?'

"There was an instance one day when he couldn't make up his mind on a chip shot. He leaned on his caddie to make the club selection. A frigging chip shot, a few feet off the green. The caddie made the call and then Purtzer hit a poor chip. He turned to the caddie and shouted, 'Wrong club.' It's remarkable to me that a great player of that caliber can't make decisions himself. He's just one of those guys who can't take responsibility for anything out there."

Anthony Wilds, who caddies for David Peoples, echoed

Medziak's opinion. "That's Purtzer's reputation for sure among us caddies," said Wilds. "In those rare instances when David misses a tournament and I'm looking for a bag, I won't consider Purtzer or others like him. All we caddies can do for our players is offer advice and maybe be a calming influence. The player has to swing the club. It's his name on the bag, not mine."

Several caddies mentioned Mike Donald as one who dislikes the bag-toters. "He claims they are overpaid and underworked," said a caddie. "Some of us said that if he had won the U.S. Open [in 1990 when Donald finished second], it would have set caddying back too far to recover in our lifetime." Added another caddie, "Mike is not a bad guy off the course. But once he steps foot on the grass, he's a jerk. That's why no one ever stays with him."

Money Bags

There are very few wealthy caddies.

Toting bags for Tour players is a vocation with no job security, benefits, or pension. It's a line of work where the wages are based solely on someone else's performance.

If they have a "regular bag" and work for the same golfer every week, they can make a six-figure income (as long as their man is a tournament winner).

A caddie earns three hundred to five hundred dollars a week, plus a percentage of a player's purse, usually up to 10 percent if the player wins. That's fine if you're carrying the bag for a top money-winner. But it can be hell if you're stuck with a loser. Weekly expenses for a caddie—food, lodging, and transportation—can run from five hundred to a thousand dollars a week.

"If your player misses the cut, you lose money," said caddie Joe LaCava. "You can't live on that kind of salary. But if you get the right bag, you can make a great living."

LaCava, who caddies mostly for Fred Couples, earned over $200,000 in 1992. "I feel very fortunate," said LaCava, who began caddying right after graduating from college with a finance degree. He toted for his cousin, Ken Green, for three years before having the good fortune to carry Couples's bag just when the golfer hit his prime as one of the world's best.

Bruce Edwards caddied for Tom Watson for seventeen years at the height of Watson's career. Edwards once received a $25,000 motor home from Watson as a Christmas present. In 1990, Edwards earned more than $200,000 lugging Greg Norman's bag. (Edwards quit as Norman's caddie and returned to his longtime employer Watson in 1992. Wouldn't you know, Norman won the Canadian Open in his first tournament with a new caddie.)

Fanny Sunesson, who caddies for Nick Faldo, reportedly is guaranteed $60,000 a year.

But for every Sunesson, Edwards, and LaCava out on the Tour, there are hundreds more who lead a nomadic life, traveling from one Tour stop to the next, standing outside the club entrance, asking the pros if they need a caddie.

LaCava got his job with a little luck and perseverance. He heard that Couples was looking for a caddie, so LaCava approached him, made his pitch, and gave him his phone number. Couples had picked someone from Europe to be his regular bag-toter, but then that caddie decided not to come to the United States. Just before the start of the 1990 season, Couples called LaCava and asked him to spend a week with him at his house in Palm Springs, California.

"It worked out great because I got to know Fred real well right away," LaCava said. "We hit it off because we both love sports and we're both laid back."

LaCava, who carries about forty weeks a year, says that to be a good caddie, you must have a rapport with your golfer.

"Fred and I don't get nervous about much," he said.

"Our philosophy is whatever happens, happens. And I don't try to be a cheerleader. Fred doesn't like to talk about golf during a round. He's more interested in sports."

Jeff "Squeeky" Medlen, a squeaky-voiced former steel-worker, is another one of the highly paid caddies on tour after forming a special bond with Nick Price in 1990. Fortunately for his pocketbook, Medlen was with Price every step of the way as the golfer finished seventh or higher on the money list over the next three seasons.

Talk about luck. In 1991, when Price withdrew from the PGA Championship because his pregnant wife was overdue, Medlen was hired by John Daly at Price's suggestion. Daly won and Medlen pocketed $23,000 for the caddie's share of the winnings. (Hours after Daly's stunning victory, Price reportedly phoned Medlen and, half in jest, made the caddie pledge his allegiance to the golfer.)

The next year, Medlen fattened his wallet some more when Price won the PGA Championship. In 1993, Squeeky earned about $125,000 toting Price's clubs.

"Some of the caddies kid me because I've been getting some press," said Medlen. "But I'm not a celebrity. However, I've done okay. I couldn't have done it without Nick."

Oops!

Caddies can have off days the same as golfers can.

Veteran caddie Paul Jungman said he once made a couple of silly mistakes that left him mortified and his golfer fit to be tied.

"I was caddying for David Canipe [an Orlando pro] one day. He had made a bogey on the 17th because I had talked him out of a club and he had come up short on the shot. He wanted to bury my ass right there on the tee. He was barking at me because I deserved it.

"That's when I looked up at him and said, 'David, if you

think you're mad at me now, just wait until I tell you this: I don't have your driver in my bag.' Either he or I had left it leaning against the water cooler on the previous hole. He was really pissed now. But while I hauled ass to find his driver, he took another club and hit it pretty good and made par. But boy was he barking at me."

■

The caddie for Senior PGA Tour player Kermit Zarley wound up all wet during the first round of the 1993 GTE Suncoast Classic.

He had parked the golf cart near the 9th green and placed Zarley's bag upright on the floor of the passenger's side before joining the golfer on the green. That's when the fun began. The golf bag toppled over and fell on the accelerator, which sent the driverless cart careening toward a nearby pond.

The caddie raced after the cart, but couldn't catch up to it before it splashed into the water. The embarrassed caddie waded into the pond and retrieved the waterlogged golf bag. While the gallery—and even Zarley—laughed, the red-faced caddie dried off the golfer's clubs.

The slapstick incident didn't distract Zarley, who shot a one-under-par 70 for the round.

■

Of all the clubs in his golf bag, only one is priceless to Tour pro Greg Kraft—an Arnold Palmer Wilson putter that was once his grandfather's.

Kraft has instructed his caddie that if ever the golf bag is left unattended, the caddie must always take the putter with him, even for just a minute. Two days before the start of the 1994 British Open at Turnberry, Todd Blersch, Kraft's caddie for more than a year, left the bag on the putting green and dutifully took the putter with him when he went to buy lunch. Blersch returned with his hamburger, but accidentally left the coveted putter behind, propped up against the side of the concession stand. When he realized his mistake, the caddie raced back to the stand, but the putter was gone.

When he mustered up the courage to tell Kraft what had happened, Blersch's job was gone too.

Said Kraft, as he prepared for the British Open, "Todd asked me if he'd ever be able to work for me again, and I said, 'I don't know. I'm so upset I can't stand it. To lose the putter two days before my first major is devastating.'

"I know it was an accident and accidents happen and I know he felt bad. But it was hard for me to deal with the fact that it was lost so carelessly.

"It was tough to fire him. He looked at me with those puppy-dog eyes. But I know if I missed a putt on the course, I'd look at him and all I'd be able to think about would be that he lost my putter."

Kraft hired a new caddie, Terry Holt. Meanwhile, the golfer appealed to the public through the news media for help in finding his lost putter. During the first two rounds of the Open, Kraft used a Ping Zing from the exhibition tent and shot 69 and 74 with five three-putts.

But before the third round, Kraft got the news that he so desperately wanted to hear—his cherished putter had been found. An unnamed spectator had handed it to a marshal at the end of the second round.

It was an emotional reunion in the R&A offices. "It was like making a hundred-footer for a win to see that putter again," said Kraft, who admitted he was near tears when it was returned. "I was so excited. I don't know if I'd ever have been able to get over it if it hadn't been turned in."

Kraft went out and struck thirty putts in a round that included five birdies and just one bogey. "That putter is irreplaceable," said Kraft. "It's so important to have a putter you feel confident you can hole putts with. It takes pressure off your whole game and you can just relax and play your best."

Burger Ball

Irish golfer David Feherty once teed off from a half-eaten hamburger because of his caddie.

"I'd been out at St. Mellion [Ireland's notoriously rugged course] for four hours," he recalled. "That's like spending four days anywhere else.

"We had to wait on the 16th tee. I was hungry, so I told my caddie to go get me a burger. The trouble is, he's a big eater.

"When I stepped up for my tee shot, I knew if I handed the burger to him, it would be an ex-burger. So I pinned it to the ground with a tee and hit my shot off it. I didn't mind if I lost my ball, but I certainly didn't want to lose my burger."

My Caddie, My Friend

In 1994, Lee Trevino refused to let his longtime caddie work any more for him—hoping it would save the caddie's life.

Herman Mitchell had been toting Trevino's bag since 1977. For years, the two have bantered back and forth on the course. Mitchell, a huge man, would glower at the five-foot-seven star and chide the golfer whenever he wasn't playing well. "You're playing like a dog," Mitchell would say. "You're not getting steak for dinner. You should go to McDonald's."

In early March 1994, Mitchell, a 321-pound, fifty-six-year-old diabetic, became ill, but refused to seek help. So Trevino took charge and personally brought Mitchell to the hospital in San Antonio. "He almost died," recalled the golfer. "He spent two weeks in the hospital there and they found out he had an enlarged heart and a weak heart muscle."

Mitchell was transferred to Duke University Medical Center, where he was placed on a special diet. "The doctors said that if we get a hundred pounds off him, he might have a shot at a few more years," said Trevino. "I told him he wasn't getting the bag back until he got down to 225 pounds. It was the only control I had. I was trying to save his life.

"He's my buddy. He's family."

Mitchell lost seventy-five pounds in three months. Only then, after he promised to stay on a strict diet and take care of himself, did Trevino allow his good buddy to carry the golfer's bag again.

■

During a tournament, Lee Trevino was verbally riding Mitchell more than usual. Although the two were always bantering back and forth, on this day Trevino was in rare form and really dishing it out.

As the golfer and caddie left the green for the next tee, a woman in the gallery asked Mitchell, "Does he always treat you this way?"

"No, ma'am," Mitchell replied. "Today is one of his better days."

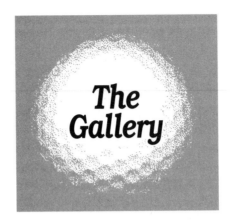

The Gallery

Put Down a Double Bogey for the Fans

Fans are getting more pushy and obnoxious on and off the course, complain the pros.

Long gone are the days of quiet reverence and polite applause. Now, galleries are not only seen but heard as well. These days, pro golf has taken on a circuslike atmosphere—and not everyone is happy about it.

"Golf used to be a gentleman's sport for both players and fans," said one golfer. "Today, for every decent golf fan there's another who's there only to party, drink, and maybe heckle us on the course."

Tom Watson said he really began noticing a change in the general behavior of the gallery at the 1992 Western Open. "I had three or four drunks following me around," he recalled. "They were really noisy, and it was frustrating, especially for the other players. But that's just a lack of etiquette. Booze does strange things to minds.

"The Masters has been the epitome of a golf tournament. Now the galleries there show a lot of partisanship [especially against European players]. That's not needed and shouldn't be encouraged.

"I just don't want something to happen like the gallery deflecting a ball or yelling on a backswing. The galleries all over are becoming more vociferous. They are not showing the etiquette of silence they used to."

Davis Love III says he's concerned over the increasing rowdiness of fans at tournaments. "It's the same people who are going to football and baseball games," he said. "They think you're supposed to yell and scream. Golf has always had the most courteous crowds of any sport, but that's changing. People are realizing they can be heard on television if they're the first ones that yell after a guy hits a shot. We're going to have to get used to it rather than hoping it changes because I don't think it'll ever change."

Occasionally fans have heckled the South African players because of the racial policies of the South African government.

Recalled South African Fulton Allem, "At [the Nestlé Invitational in] Bay Hill, I was tied for the lead and right in the middle of my backswing when some guy in the gallery swore at me and called me a racist SOB and told me to go back to South Africa.

"Later, he was in the clubhouse restaurant and bar, watching the action on television, not realizing he was sitting next to my wife. When I made a bogey, he said, 'Thank God they've got that racist SOB off the board.' A few minutes later, he asked [Allem's wife] Colleen whose wife she was. She wouldn't tell him.

"When I came into the restaurant after the round, a friend of mine pointed him out and I confronted him about what he had said to me on the course, but he denied it. I was holding a Coke in my hand so I just poured it over his head. If it had happened a few years earlier, I would've nailed him."

Antiapartheid protesters also have pestered Nick Price on the course. Although he was irked, he didn't tee off on them. Instead, he sought them out and explained that although he was born in Durban, South Africa, he moved to Zimbabwe (formerly Rhodesia) at age two. And he's always carried a British passport. Not only that but he lives in Orlando, Florida.

Australian Craig Parry held the third-round lead at the 1992 Masters with a twelve-under-par 204 before skying to a final-round 78 and a tie for thirteenth place. Although he didn't blame his collapse on rowdy fans, Parry said they distracted him by behaving rudely toward him because he wasn't an American.

"They were rooting against me," he told reporters afterward. "They even coughed during my putts. I'll be wearing a Walkman next year."

Fans can be cruel to Americans as well. After overcoming a suspension to get his life back in order, recovering alcoholic John Daly received tremendous support from fans. Unfortunately, his ears got blistered from crass, insensitive gallery goons who would heckle him about his past drinking problem.

Recalled Daly, "I'd hear someone yell, 'Why don't you start drinking again? You'll play better.' That was the worst one. It hurt for a little bit. I let that bother me at first, but not anymore. Now I just ignore it."

That's about all the pros can do. In the pro-am at the 1993 Buick Open, Billy Andrade topped a tee shot. As the golfer muttered to himself, a spectator snickered and yelled, "Hey, Billy, real nice. Two or three more like that and you might reach the green."

Instinctively, Andrade wheeled around and was about to blurt out a nasty retort when he caught himself. "There was no point," he recalled. "If I said something back, I would be the bad guy."

After the round, a couple of spectators approached Andrade and thanked him for his self-control. "It turns out the guy had severe learning disabilities," said Andrade. "He was a grown man, but had the IQ of a child and he didn't completely understand what he was saying. I would have felt awful if I had ripped the guy."

After tennis star Monica Seles was stabbed and figure skater Nancy Kerrigan was attacked, golfers on tour are more concerned than ever about the possibilities of fan violence on the course.

"There's no way to stop a nut from going after you if he wants to," claims Greg Norman. "The crowd is so close to you that you don't stand much of a chance."

Lee Trevino doesn't quite share Norman's view. "If you're going to try to do something to golfers, bring something more than a knife or stick," he said. "Golfers have weapons called golf clubs."

Who are the gallery hounds who play to the crowd?

Lee Trevino
Chi Chi Rodriguez
Peter Jacobsen
John Daly
Billy Andrade
Mark O'Meara
Fuzzy Zoeller
Payne Stewart
Seve Ballesteros

Sign of the Times

An increasing number of pros believe fans are becoming more aggressive when asking players for autographs.

"At the U.S. Open, it was the most incredible press of people trying to get to players," Hale Irwin recalled. "It was actually scary. We were walking with policemen that had flak jackets on. When one fan runs toward a golfer, they all start running. It can become a stampede.

"It's not that unusual anymore to have kids or adults screaming and hollering for your autograph after you've already said no once and politely asked them to be quiet."

Many golfers who used to sign autographs willingly admit they're less obliging today.

"It used to be that I'd sign fifteen autographs during a round," said Fred Couples. "Now you have fifty people on every hole. A lot of people don't understand when you tell them, 'I can't sign now but I will when I'm finished.' Then, when you're walking off the course, people are pushing and shoving. I get uptight.

"You can't sign every autograph. I'd love to sign as many as possible, but I'm out there to play and practice."

After Nick Price won the 1992 PGA Championship, "requests for my autograph quadrupled," he said. "What's even more amazing was that Squeek [his caddie Jeff Medlen] was signing autographs too."

Price says that during a typical tournament, he signs about a thousand autographs. But he's not complaining. "It's nice when people want your autograph," he explained.

Jim Gallagher Jr. says he gives about five hundred signatures a week during a tournament. "I'll sign as many as I can," he said. "My problem is, I stop walking to sign. I'll sign as long as I have the time. I hate to run off on a little kid."

Other golfers are developing a bad attitude toward fans, said one pro. "Some of the big names on tour do everything they can to avoid signing autographs," he claimed. "They have security guards clearing a path for them. Sometimes you can understand it when the crowds get too unruly. But often, these guys just don't want to take the time to sign."

Irwin says the pros appreciate the fans, but there's a limit to how much time the golfers can spend with them.

"Arnold Palmer and Jack Nicklaus handle it extremely well," said Irwin. "But you can only sign so many autographs. If you sign fifty, you disappoint five hundred. How do you say no politely?"

Watson hopes fans will understand that it's impossible for players to sign every autograph request. "I just tell people, 'I can't sign right now, thank you.' And I try to concentrate on the little kids. They're the ones you get the big smiles from. They're who I like to do things for."

When the issue of golfers' responsibility toward fans was raised recently at the PGA Championship, Jack Nicklaus lashed out publicly at the stars who go out of their way not to sign autographs.

"Grow up," Nicklaus said. "I mean, c'mon. If you play the game, it's part of the heat, isn't it? If you win major championships, you have to deal with it. Palmer, Watson, and Trevino have dealt with it for years. It's part of the game."

Fandemonium

It's almost unanimous among the Tour players: Nobody handles the fans on or off the course better than Arnold Palmer.

"Palmer is the greatest at what he does with fans," says Mark O'Meara. "He knows how to deal with people. He's probably the greatest people person in the history of golf.

"He might be one of the most famous persons in our sport, but I've never seen him be snobby to anybody. He treats Joe Blow the same way he treats any guy in his foursome at the U.S. Open."

Lee Trevino says he's amazed at how gracious Palmer is when fans bug him.

"I've never seen Palmer refuse to sign an autograph," said Trevino. "I've seen him having dinner at a restaurant, the poor guy, and they [fans] get chairs and set them around at his table while his food is in front of him. They're taking pictures and everything.

"What that's done to me is make me a hermit. You very seldom see me go out in public. I don't even go to the grocery store with my wife because she won't go in with me. She says, 'You sit in the car. I can get more done without you.'

"When I'm home, we never go out to dinner. We eat at home. On tour, I have room service probably more than anyone else who has ever stayed in a hotel. It's nothing for me to eat room service six nights in a row when I'm alone. I haven't been in a bar in over fifteen years to have a drink with friends because they [fans] come up and start bothering you.

"Everybody seems to put you on a pedestal because you do something very well. A lot of the people lose sight of the fact that you are human and like your privacy.

"You give 1,000 percent out here to thirty thousand people and when you leave, you really are exhausted. That would be like a performer going on stage and doing a two-hour concert and then coming back and sitting in the audience."

When he's done being a golfing celebrity for the day, Trevino says, he has a right not to answer questions, pose for pictures, or sign autographs.

"I don't want to sign an autograph when I get into a hotel elevator. When I've got my family with me or I'm at the dinner table after I've been out on the course and it's been a tough day, I don't want to go to another guy's table and say hello to his grandmother and take a picture with her. I think that I have given enough of myself."

Fuzzy Zoeller wants to put autograph seekers in perspective: "Without those people behind those ropes, we have nothing. We wouldn't have the charity donations that we have now. There would be a lot of lost causes out there, a lot of sad faces. I accept the fact that the fans are my boss. They pay my way and I appreciate them doing it. So, of course, I'm nice to them."

Win a Major, Lose Your Privacy

Winning the 1992 U.S. Open not only changed Tom Kite's life, it affected the life of his family.

Whenever his wife Christy and kids, Stephanie, twelve, and nine-year-old twins Paul and David, attended a tournament, they would gather outside the scorer's tent and wait for Tom after the round. However, since winning the Open, Kite gets besieged by autograph seekers as soon as he signs his scorecard.

"The kids were used to going up to him after he finished a round," says Christy. "Now they can't get near him. That doesn't set too well with them."

At tournament time, there are more distractions than before, such as extra dinners, network interviews, press conferences, and media check-ins.

"When you shoot even par, you're usually not going to be stopped by writers," Christy said. "Now he has reporters talking to him after almost every round."

Even though Kite has been seen on television for years, public recognition has increased enormously since winning the Open, she said. After struggling through two rounds of the 1993 Masters with a pair of herniated disks in his back, Kite took some time off from the Tour.

"We went out to dinner one night and three people we'd never met came up to tell Tom what doctor to go see for his back," said Christy. "Our private life is definitely not as private as it once was."

Although Kite finds that most everyone wants a piece of his time, he tries to remain the same person he's always been, says good friend Davis Love III. "He's not one to think he's a big celebrity or a hotshot. He doesn't fall into the trap of thinking about the money or the contracts or the fame."

■

How did the fans treat Paul Azinger after he won his first major, the 1993 PGA Championship?

"Now when I go to get gas for my boat, the guy with the tattoos recognizes me," said the Zinger, weeks after the victory.

"As far as how fans treat me, my life definitely has changed. I have more mail than I can possibly answer. It all really sank in when I was walking through the Mirage casino in Las Vegas. I was mobbed. It was unbelievable."

Fair-Weather Fairway Fans

When Jeff Maggert nailed a double eagle on the par-5, 485-yard 13th hole in the final round of the 1994 Masters, his wife Kelli missed it—because of two jerks in the gallery.

Recalled Kelli, "Just before Jeff hit his shot, these guys were standing in front of me and one said, 'Who is this Jeff Maggert? He's no good.' It made me angry, so I wasn't watching his shot.

"Then, all of a sudden, I heard this roar, so I went back to these two guys and said, 'What do you think of him now?'

"One of them replied, 'Jeff Maggert is a great golfer.'"

■

Female fans let Ian Baker-Finch know they think he's one of the most handsome players on the Tour.

"It's more the moms and the older ladies who give me a hard time," the Australian says with a blush. "They'll say, 'Isn't he gorgeous?' Or 'I wish I were ten years younger because I'd ask him out.'

"It gets to be a bit much when you bend over to line up a putt, and a lady whistles.

"I've had women pull their shirts out and say, 'Sign here, please' [on their tummies]. I've been asked to sign certain places like the chest or the butt. I do sign the occasional butt or chest."

■

In the first round of the 1993 Vantage Classic at Tanglewood Golf Club in Clemmons, North Carolina, Senior PGA Tour rookie Jerry McGee was one under at the turn.

On the 10th tee, he pulled his drive into the rough. It didn't look like it would pose much of a problem. But even though McGee and his caddie were sure where the ball landed, they couldn't find it.

Some fans claimed a witless female spectator swiped the ball, but there was no proof. As a result, McGee had to treat the situation as a lost ball, so he returned to the tee and, because of the penalty, drove his third shot. He wound up with a double-bogey six.

"That's never happened to me before in all the years I've played," said McGee, who finished the tournament in a tie for twelfth. Without the penalty strokes, he would have finished in a ninth-place tie and earned $12,000 more.

"If I ever find the lady who took my ball, I'll autograph it and let her keep it—if she'll reimburse me for the money I lost with those extra strokes."

**Which tournament
has the worst crowds?**

Buick Classic, Westchester CC, Rye, N.Y.
Ryder Cup
AT&T Pebble Beach National Pro-Am
Phoenix Open
Kmart Greater Greensboro Open

Pen Pals

While John Daly was walking to the final hole at the 1994 Merrill Lynch Shoot-Out in Greensboro, a little boy shyly asked Long John to autograph his hat.

Bending down, Daly asked the little boy, "What's your name?"

"Zachary," he replied.

"Well, Zachary, I'll give you my autograph if you'll give me yours." And so they swapped signatures, much to the delight of the crowd.

High Jinks on the Links

Ask the pros who has been the top gallery hound over the last few decades and two words tumble off their lips: Chi Chi.

For almost thirty years, Chi Chi Rodriguez has delighted millions of golf fans with his antics on the course such as covering the hole with his Panama hat or pretending his putter is a sword.

"Americans are so hard-working and half of them don't enjoy their work," he said. "So I try to give them something to smile about. Golf is show business and I love making people laugh."

But not many pros were laughing when Rodriguez first showed up on the PGA scene in 1960. He was branded a hotdog by many of the players and actually fined by sourpuss officials for "conduct unbecoming a professional golfer" after one too many fun-loving stunts on the course.

However, what stung Chi Chi the most was when his idol, Arnold Palmer, chastised him at the 1964 Masters for goofing around.

"I thought he was picking on me," Rodriguez recalled. "I was very much hurt. I went to the locker room and cried.

Later, I realized that if I wasn't wrong, Arnold never would have said anything."

So Chi Chi toned down his act, showed respect for the Tour, and yet still remained a fan favorite.

"Call me a clown, call me a nice guy," he said. "Just don't call me collect."

**Which tournament
has the best crowds?**

British Open
The Masters
Ryder Cup
Players Championship
Nissan Los Angeles Open
Phoenix Open
U.S. Open
GTE Byron Nelson Classic

Elementary, My Dear Watson

As he prepared for the 1994 Masters, Tom Watson—a notorious streak putter—received unsolicited putting tips from fans across the country.

For example, fans sent him such things as:

• a homemade video of a fan demonstrating putting techniques;

• six used putters;

• an instruction booklet authored by Watson himself with a note to "reread this";

• tape to put around his pinky finger;

• letters telling him how to improve his putting.

Watson used his putter well at the Masters and finished a respectable thirteenth.

Public Image

Getting to Know You

Many players aren't like their public image.

Steve Pate's nickname is "The Human Volcano." But he's not like that image, according to Larry Rinker. "Everybody sees Steve erupting, but he's really a nice guy," says Rinker.

Craig Stadler is another player who doesn't quite fit his image, says Donnie Hammond. "Craig always looks like he's ready to strangle somebody," said Hammond. "But then he wants to have a hot dog with you after the round."

Mark McCumber agrees that Stadler doesn't show his true self in public. "Craig is really a good guy. I know he doesn't come across to the public that way because he always has that scowl on his face."

Stadler simply doesn't let people outside of the golf world see how nice he is, says Brad Bryant. "His public image is that of the gruff, hot-tempered guy. But I haven't found him to be that way at all. I love him to death."

Paul Azinger has a reputation for being funny and laid back. But he's also very intense, says Peter Jacobsen. "For a guy who comes wrapped up in such a nice, warm package, he has a fire that could light up a whole city.

"More than anything, he smashes the stereotype that nice guys finish last. He's one of the nicest guys out here, but he might be the best of all of us."

Azinger believes that his good friend Payne Stewart is misjudged because of his volatile, emotional nature. "He's so misunderstood by people who have never had the chance to be around him," said Azinger. "He's got the greatest sense of humor and he's got a heart of pure gold. No one in the world enjoys a good laugh like he does. Payne is really a kid at heart, and you've got to be that way to survive out here with all the pressure that goes on with this profession. I wish the world could see him the way he really is."

Corey Pavin has a reputation for arrogance, yet he's considered one of the nicer guys on tour.

"I'm a pretty private person," he says. "I don't express all of my emotions to people. Sometimes that gets interpreted as cockiness or arrogance. I guess I've put some walls around myself."

Andrew Magee wanted to do something to change his nice-guy image on the course.

He was watching a baseball game on television one day when he noticed that many of the best relief pitchers—the intimidating ones—have that scruffy, unshaven look.

So he grew a goatee and began playing more aggressive golf—and in 1994 won his first tournament in two years.

"I thought the goatee would give me a tougher feeling," he explained. "I see relief pitchers who never shave go into these really tense situations and pull it out. I like their style."

The Name Game

• Simon Hobday is nicknamed "Scruffy." That's because the likeable South African who won the 1994 U.S. Senior

Open has been accused of buying his clothes at Ringling Brothers.

Knowing that his fashion sense is the antithesis of *Gentleman's Quarterly,* Hobday claims he once asked a clothing manufacturer for $500,000 for *not* wearing the company's line of golf shirts.

• Brad Bryant is often called "Dr. Dirt." Not that the veteran golfer is unclean. It's just that he has a five o'clock shadow by noon and a reputation for wearing wrinkled clothes because of his aversion to dry cleaning. (He bought his first pair of dry-clean-only pants in 1994 and promptly declared, "I hate them.")

Gary McCord was the first to call Bryant "Mr. Dirt" after a character in a Mobil gasoline commercial in the early 1980s. But the moniker was soon upgraded to "Dr. Dirt." Says Bryant, who wears the name like a badge of honor, "The nickname fits me. I'm a country boy at heart and my family were farmers. When they heard about my nickname, they thought it was great."

• John Huston is good-naturedly called "Swamp Thing." During the 1993 Honda Classic at Weston Hills Country Club in Fort Lauderdale, Huston hit his tee shot on the 7th hole into the lake and accidentally sent his driver sailing in there too.

But rather than let his driver rest in peace, Huston removed his shoes and socks, rolled up his pants and waded in after it. There was only one problem. The lake bottom was extremely soft. Huston began to sink, first to his knees, then his thighs, next his waist, and finally all the way up to his chest. Fortunately, he managed to escape the muddy grasp.

When he returned to the tee, Huston dumped another shot into the water and went on to make a very soggy and memorable quintuple bogey 10. Since then, Huston has been known among his fellow golfers on the Tour as "Swamp Thing."

• Payne Stewart was first called "Avis" in the mid-1980s for his propensity to finish second.

In 1986, he finished third on the money list without winning a tournament. The nickname began to fade when he won two majors, one in 1989 and another in 1991. But the moniker resurfaced in 1993 when Stewart finished second in four tournaments.

• Greg Norman got the nickname the "Great White Shark" at the 1981 Masters. Norman, a twenty-six-year-old Aussie who wasn't even a member of the PGA Tour yet, was battling for the lead after the second round. During an interview in the press room, Norman said he loved to fish for sharks.

"The next morning in the *Augusta Chronicle* is this headline, 'Great White Shark Near Masters Lead.'" Norman recalled. "I don't know who wrote it but he made a hell of a lot of money for me. It's been a wonderful logo. I love the image. The blond hair, the aggressive style, it all fits together."

When he's played poorly, some of his fellow golfers have mockingly referred to him as "The Great White Carp."

Snickers for Those Knickers

Payne Stewart's colorful cap-and-knickers ensemble make him one of the most instantly recognizable personalities on the golf course.

The most famous wardrobe in golf was born at the 1982 Atlanta Classic when Stewart was hitting balls on the practice range. He saw six players dressed exactly as he was—in red golf slacks, white shirt, and white shoes.

"I vowed right then I was not going to be another look-alike golfer," recalled Stewart. "I didn't know what I was going to do differently, but I knew there had to be something."

He thought about his father Bill, a salesman for a furniture manufacturer who made his calls outfitted in out-landishly loud sport coats. Sometimes, Bill would deliber-ately dress in clothes that didn't match just so his cus-tomers would never forget him. "Dad always said, 'If you stand out when you go in to sell somebody something, they will always remember who you are. If you go in dressed in boring navy blue, you're just somebody in the crowd.'

"As I continued to look at those golfers on the practice green, I remembered how nice some of the players looked in knickers on the Asian Tour [which he played before earning his PGA Tour card in 1981], so I decided to give knickers a shot."

It took him about an hour to develop a thick skin over the gibes and jokes from other golfers about his knickers. It was just his luck that he was paired with Lee Trevino. "Oh, did Lee have a great time cracking jokes at my expense," recalled Stewart. "He wouldn't let up the whole round."

But Stewart refused to nix the knickers. A few weeks later, he won his first PGA tournament—the Quad Cities Open, where he wore knickers in all four rounds. A tradi-tion of unique fashion was born.

"Knickers are good for my golf game," Stewart claims. "They're cooler in hot weather because the air circulates in them and they're warmer in cold weather because they trap the body heat."

Stewart, who has a twenty-foot-long closet that's barely big enough to hold all his knickers, says he wishes other golfers would take a little more time in picking out their clothes in the morning. "We do have a dress code out here. But sometimes I think it's ignored."

Of course, not everyone appreciates Stewart's fashion sense. In fact, during a practice round at the Honda Clas-sic in 1992, his good friend and fellow pro Paul Azinger was joking about Stewart's knickers to some women in the gallery. "Ladies," said Azinger, "how could you like a guy who dresses like a clown?"

Moments later, the women hustled over to Stewart, who was on the other side of a lake, and told him what Azinger had said. Stewart then pulled out a six-iron and aimed a shot at his buddy across the water. He should have used a wedge. The ball sailed over Azinger's head and landed in the gallery. "Oops," said Stewart. "I shouldn't have done that. But Zinger had it coming."

■

One of the benefits of having a unique uniform is that Stewart is less recognizable to the casual fan when the golfer is wearing regular clothes off the course.

"It's so much easier for me to walk around in public than it is for a lot of guys on tour," he said. "It's very rare that I'm recognized because people don't know me in a regular shirt and slacks."

How much money would it take for you to dress like Payne Stewart?

Tom Kite: "It would be more like, 'What would they have to threaten me with?' They'd have to take my wife and kids. They couldn't pay me enough money."

Lee Janzen: "Twice as much as they offer him."

Joey Sindelar: "It's not possible."

Ernie Els: "Bazillions."

Hal Sutton: "A lot. I just wouldn't wear knickers."

Fulton Allem: "Not a whole lot. I just don't have the body for it."

The Good, the Bad, and the Ugly

To some players, pro-ams are a chore. To others, they are a ball.

Many of these events are one-day affairs held before a tournament. The Tour also includes four pro-ams in which the pros and amateurs compete together. The odd couples are paired for every round but the final one.

Many pros complain they can't concentrate when they are playing in the company of eighteen-handicappers and trying to be sociable.

Bob Lohr likes pro-ams, although he understands why some of his fellow pros are less enthused. "The reason most guys don't like the pro-am format is the speed of the play," said Lohr. "If amateurs who are out of the hole would simply pick up, it would help play move along. But some of them feel as though they need to hit every shot—no matter how far in the woods it is—to get their money's worth.

"I've seen some important people—CEOs of major companies—do things in a pro-am that you absolutely would not believe. But there's none I'd want to see in print."

Although Blaine McCallister says he likes pro-ams, there is a downside. "If I have a problem with them, it's that I sometimes find myself trying extra hard to make sure the amateurs have a good time," he said. "I shouldn't worry about that because then I'm not focused. If I'm not focused and I play poorly, it could make for a long day for the amateurs."

Many pros have mixed feelings about the pro-am event at the Las Vegas Invitational. "It's the best because it's Vegas, the gaming tables, the shows, and the night life," said one golfer. "It's the worst because of the pro-am.

"Many of the amateurs are invited simply because of the amount of money they lose at the tables. Some of them don't know anything about golf and it makes for a very long day for everybody. Sometimes a guy will come in and play the first couple of rounds, then maybe drop a bundle at the tables on the second night, catch a plane, and blow off his final round. That really screws things up for the tournament."

Says Payne Stewart, "There's a concern among some of the veteran pros about how we act and how we treat our pro-am partners. A lot of the pros treat it with the attitude of 'Let's just get it over with.'

"But it's something we need to concentrate on, to make it a special day for the guys we play with. Those are the guys who are buying sponsorships and really supporting our Tour with their wallets. We have to treat them with a special kind of respect.

"We have to make sure they enjoy their day because if we don't, they aren't going to keep paying their two thousand dollars or whatever to play with us. We certainly can't afford for them to go back and tell their friends or the company they work for that we pros are jerks.

"We have to keep impressing upon the younger players how important these pro-ams are to us."

Adds David Peoples, "I really don't have any complaints. You know, playing professional golf is a nice job and I feel very privileged to be here. It does kind of irk me when I hear the younger guys complaining about the money at the pro-ams. I just want to shake these guys and say, 'Look, buddy, do you know how good we have it? We're playing for a million dollars a week.' "

Says Mark O'Meara, "There's nothing wrong with going out and playing a round of golf with a bunch of nice guys who care enough about playing with you that they put up some pretty big money for the privilege.

"I thoroughly enjoy playing with the amateurs. Maybe it's because I remember not so long ago when I was an amateur, and I know what a big thrill it would have been for me to play in a tournament with a PGA pro. It would have meant so much."

During pro-ams, Lee Trevino claims, he goes out of his way to make sure his playing partners are having a good time.

"I'm going to entertain the crowd," says Trevino. "I'm playing with four amateurs who paid a lot of money to hook up with me. I'll give them 1,000 percent.

"When I play in pro-ams, it's not a day for me. It's a day for my amateur partners. I like to read the putts for them, cheer for them, and let them gave a good time. I will help them have a day in the sun."

Senior PGA player Dave Stockton says he tries to help his amateur partners by giving them golf tips. "I want every single amateur I play with to walk home with something that will help his golf game," he said. "During the course of the round, I'll try and help him with his long or short game. Most of the time, my thinking is on the mental part. For instance, I'll ask him why he has chosen a certain club. In a nutshell, I want the amateurs to walk off the 18th green having had an enjoyable experience and leaving with something that will benefit them in the future."

What's the strangest thing that's ever happened to you in a pro-am?

Mark McCumber: "One time in Jacksonville, I played with an amateur who hit a chip shot that looked a little short. I yelled, 'Get up! Get up!' and it ran past the hole. The amateur then turned to me and said, 'Hey, get your mouth off my ball!'"

Willie Wood: "I was playing with Jamie Farr [the actor who played cross-dressing Corporal Klinger in the TV series "M*A*S*H"]. His second shot on the very first hole went dead left off the heel of the club and hit my caddie right in the head. The shot knocked him out cold. Then there was the time in the Mexican Open when an amateur hit a shot that bounced off a tree and went right between my legs really hard. Boy, was that scary!"

Kenny Knox: "One of my partners hit a ball under an ambulance [at the 1992 Canon Greater Hartford Open]. They had to move it so he could hit the shot. I thought when he got there, he might just climb in, but he didn't."

If Only All the Tournaments Could Be Pro-Ams

Mark O'Meara loves pro-ams.

No wonder. Five of his eight PGA Tour victories have come in pro-am events.

"They call me the king of the pro-ams," said the veteran. He has won four titles at the AT&T Pebble Beach National Pro-Am and one at the 1991 Walt Disney World/Oldsmobile Classic. In addition, he has finished second in three other pro-am tournaments.

"I actually do better when I'm with the amateur players," said O'Meara. "It has a lot to do with the tedium of actually playing in a tournament. Some guys [on the Tour] want absolutely nothing to enter their minds except their next shot. For me, it's the exact opposite.

"I find it very difficult to concentrate on my own golf game for five hours, the way we have to do in most tournaments. In the pro-am event, you settle in over your shot, and put your entire focus into that shot, and then you hit it.

"Then you put up your club and walk over to an amateur partner and concern yourself with the shot he's about to hit. It really is a good way, I think, to break up the mental pressure that can build over eighteen holes.

"Now, after all my guys have played, then I focus on my shot. I've given myself a mental break and now I can get back to my ball fresh, ready to settle in again and do what I've got to do to make my shot a good one. I find the round is a lot more fun, and I don't get so emotionally drained."

Players who grumble about pro-ams mean there are fewer golfers O'Meara has to worry about beating. That's because they will beat themselves, fretting over how to handle themselves with amateurs, he explains.

"A lot of players convince themselves before they even go out there that they don't want to spend the day with amateurs, guys with funny swings who don't play as well as the pros can. Watching bad swings from others never affects me. I've been playing golf forever. Do you think I'm going to watch one guy slash at it like a lumberjack and that will throw off my swing? Come on. That simply makes no sense."

**Courses
and
Tournaments**

Why Golfers Love Their Favorite Tournaments

Chip Beck: Las Vegas Invitational (even though it's one of the least favorite among his fellow pros). "It's not just the 59 I shot there in 1991 or the gambling and all the things that go along with Las Vegas. I always have a good time there and the people are so friendly."

Tom Purtzer: The Memorial at Muirfield Village Golf Club in Dublin, Ohio. "It's a great golf course and practice facility overall. And it's a good golf town with great fans who know their stuff."

Ernie Els: The Memorial. "The clubhouse, the practice area, the locker room, everything is great there."

Hal Sutton: The International at Castle Pines Golf Club in Castle Rock, Colorado. "The locker room, food, and scenery are all terrific."

Bill Murchison: The B.C. Open at En-Joie Golf Club in Endicott, New York. "I like the golf course and the people there are very friendly."

Phil Blackmar: The Players Championship at the TPC at Sawgrass, Ponte Vedra Beach, Florida. "We are taken real good care of by the hosts. Plus, it's the best fishing on the Tour."

Gary Koch: The MCI Heritage Classic at Harbour Town Golf Links in Hilton Head Island, South Carolina. "I love the golf course there. It's a great week for the family. We stay in great condos and there are lots of activities for the kids."

David Peoples: The Walt Disney World/Oldsmobile Classic (even though it's one of the least favorite among his fellow pros). "I get a chance to take my kids out to the park and spend time with them there after my round. I play in the father-son tournament. In 1993, I played with my four-year-old son and we won. That was the best I played all year." (In the real tournament, Peoples finished in a disappointing tie for sixtieth, shooting 280.)

Brad Bryant: The AT&T Pebble Beach National Pro-Am. "It's my favorite, except it is such a pain to play. There's just something special about playing Pebble Beach and Spyglass Hill.

"Also, I enjoy the GTE Byron Nelson Classic [at the TPC at Las Colinas in Irving, Texas]. They really treat you nice there and they have a wonderful golf course."

Andrew Magee: "The British Open is my favorite by far. I enjoy playing in terrible conditions. It's like playing in

---

***What are your favorite tournaments,
not including the majors
or the Players Championship?***

Memorial Tournament
Southwestern Bell Colonial
The International
Motorola Western Open
Nestlé Invitational
Nissan Los Angeles Open
Doral-Ryder Open
GTE Byron Nelson Classic
AT&T Pebble Beach National Pro-Am
MCI Heritage Classic

North Texas and Oklahoma where I grew up. I like the people. It's the purest classic golf tournament. And the beer is good in Scotland too."

Bruce Crampton: "Any course that I can win on."

What are your least favorite tournaments?

Freeport-McMoRan Classic
Kemper Open
Greater Milwaukee Open
Canon Greater Hartford Open
Las Vegas Invitational
Walt Disney World/Oldsmobile Classic
United Airlines Hawaiian Open
Honda Classic
Bob Hope Chrysler Classic
Hardee's Golf Classic (tie)
Deposit Guaranty Golf Classic (tie)

Mickey Mouse Golfers

When the pro golfer sits down at the beginning of the year to plan his schedule, there is only one stop on the Tour that his family insists he make—the Walt Disney World/Oldsmobile Classic.

"I have to commit to this one before I commit to Augusta," says Mark McCumber. "I will be going there until I join the Senior Tour."

Tom Lehman admitted that golf almost becomes a sidelight. "My kids [ages four and two] were wearing me out when we were last there," he said. "Playing golf is the easiest part of the day."

In 1993, Jeff Maggert was toying with the idea of skipping the Disney Classic for a trip to Japan. But that was before he had consulted with his two children, ages six and three. "My wife told my six year old that we might not be going," Maggert recalled. "He put his foot down. He won." It's a good thing his son put up a fuss because Maggert wound up winning the tournament.

Mark Wiebe had quite a busy schedule laid out for him when he arrived on a Sunday for the 1993 Disney Classic. His three kids made sure Dad knew the agenda: Sunday night was EPCOT, Monday was the Magic Kingdom, and Wednesday was Disney-MGM Studios. They allowed Dad a practice round of golf on Tuesday. But that evening he was expected back at the Magic Kingdom.

Veteran Hubert Green, the father of three, has a tip for newcomers to the Disney Classic: "It's simple," he said. "I always got two rooms when we came here. I had one to myself where I could rest, relax, and worry about golf. The family had the other one. They could do exactly what they wanted."

To the Victors Go the Spoiled

Players today are spoiled by tournament organizers, claim veterans Lanny Wadkins and Raymond Floyd.

"Tournaments go overboard in what they do for the players," Wadkins said. "It's great they do the things they do, but sometimes the players should be doing more things for themselves instead of depending on the tournaments for stuff like dry cleaning and baby-sitting. Some guys really take advantage of it.

"Colonial, for example, has free meals for the family for the week. There are guys who go in there and eat every meal all week—breakfast, lunch, and dinner—instead of when you just happen to be there. That's not right. It's almost like the tournaments are too nice to us."

Floyd believes that most players take the endless perks for granted.

"When I joined the Tour, we were lucky if someone told us our starting times," he said. "Today, the kids [younger pros] waltz out there expecting courtesy cars, free food, free range balls, free day-care for their children, and if something isn't perfect, they make a spectacle of themselves.

"In a sense, you can't blame them—it's the system that has engendered that sense of entitlement. I think some of the younger players need to learn some manners. And some of us older guys need to do the teaching.

"Now and then when I see a young player act up, I'll pull him aside and say, 'Think about what you did out there. Your conduct reflects not only on you but on me and the rest of the Tour as well. Think about the good fortune you have playing on the PGA Tour and the responsibilities that go with it. If you play with me again and act the way you did, I'll put a stop to it. I'll embarrass you.'"

If you had to play just one golf course for the rest of your life, what would it be?

David Feherty: "St. Andrews. It's different every time you play it. The more you play it, the more you like it."

Andrew McGee: "Cypress Point. It's beautiful, tough, fun, and scenic."

Bill Glasson: "Pebble Beach—if it's warm. It seems to have a different personality every time you play it."

Scott Simpson: "Pebble Beach. I just love it. It's a great golf course, and beautiful too."

Jim McGovern: "Augusta National. It's a great test, every shot is demanding. Every hole is scary, but there are some birdie holes."

Mark Calcavecchia: "Pebble Beach. Just because there is so much variety, weather, hazards, and beauty."

Payne Stewart: "Cypress Point. I think it is the prettiest place in the world to play golf."

Brad Bryant: "Spyglass Hill. It's such a happening course. It definitely evokes a response. I love it. You can't go around Spyglass Hill and say, 'Boy, was that a boring round of golf.'"

What is the mystique of the Masters?

Donnie Hammond: "The atmosphere at Augusta National is great and the course is beautiful, and the greens are fast, which I like. The Masters is a celebration. Just being there is fun."

Mark McCumber: "The pure environment. There's a special feeling and atmosphere about the Masters. I love everything about it from the clam chowder to the range."

Phil Mickelson: "The history. It's having a major played on the same course every year, so history is made every year. And every hole out there has had something happen that makes it special."

Davis Love III: "The front gate and the driveway. The mystique about the tournament itself is the greens. It takes so much to learn how to putt them."

Corey Pavin: "The atmosphere. It's just incredible."

Wayne Grady: "The green jacket. And it would look very good in my closet."

Oh, What a Relief It Is

After birdying the 11th hole in the second round of the 1994 Masters, Greg Norman disappeared into the trees behind the green to relieve himself.

When he returned a few minutes later, most of the spectators at the 12th tee—knowing full well why he had momentarily left the course—gave him a rousing ovation.

It's all part of the Masters tradition. According to the *Augusta Chronicle,* years ago, Arnold Palmer was heading down the 11th fairway when he walked off into the trees to answer nature's call. When he emerged from the trees and entered the fairway, the gallery cheered.

The next year, the players discovered that club chairman Clifford Roberts had built them an outhouse among the trees.

"Thankfully," Palmer told the *Chronicle,* "he didn't name it after me."

> **"If there's a golf course in heaven, I hope it's like Augusta National. I just don't want an early tee time."**
>
> —Gary Player

Escape Goats

At the TPC at Sawgrass, Pete Dye thought it would be a nice touch to have goats graze in the rough just like they do in Ireland.

But Dye and the developers were faced with some "baaad" news. The Emerald Isle may not have alligators, but Sawgrass does—hungry, goat-eating gators. The TPC got rid of what was left of the goat herd and used mowers instead.

The Pressure of the Ryder Cup Runneth Over

Almost to a man, those who have played in the Ryder Cup claim it is the most pressure-packed event in golf.

Hale Irwin, a three-time U.S. Open champion, confessed that he never felt as much pressure as he did during the deciding singles match of the 1991 Ryder Cup. "I couldn't breathe," he recalled. "I couldn't swallow. There were times when I could barely hit the ball." Despite the intense pressure, he halved the match to preserve America's 14½ to 13½ victory.

"The pressure is at an enormous pitch, more than even the players can anticipate or imagine," said Johnny Miller. "It's much more intense than at a major championship.

"The number-one source of pressure and choking is that you don't want to let your teammates down. It's the only time all year when you care more about others than yourself. It evokes strange responses in people. Playing for your country is big. But not wanting to let down your peers is bigger."

Corey Pavin was the first U.S. player to tee off in the 1993 Ryder Cup competition. Pavin admitted that he was so nervous he could barely tee his ball up because his hands were shaking. But then he told himself, "This is just the Ryder Cup, not the end of the world." He proceeded to hit a perfect drive.

John Cook, a veteran on the Tour since 1980, confessed that he never felt as nervous as he did when he went to tee off at the 1993 Ryder Cup.

"I was incredibly nervous on my first tee shot," he said. "I kind of wished I had been somewhere else at the time. That's not a feeling I'd ever had before in golf. After all, this is what we do for a living day in and day out. You get used to the pressure. But not in this case. I have never felt such pressure like I felt at that moment.

"I really just wanted to move the ball forward and get on with it. In all the years I've played professional golf, I thought I had seen and felt everything. But this was something else."

Fortunately, Cook hit a decent tee shot and he and Chip Beck went on to win a pivotal match.

"Put me into any life situation after that experience and I know I will be able to pull through it," said Cook. "The Ryder Cup experience made me a better golfer and a better person."

The pressure builds to the point where every mishit is magnified.

During the final day of the 1991 Ryder Cup, Mark Calcavecchia was 4 up with four holes to play against Colin Montgomerie. But the pressure was too great for the American. He finished with two triple bogies and two bogies, allowing Montgomerie to halve their match.

Mistakenly believing that he had cost his team the Cup, Calcavecchia fled the course in tears. "I cried," he recalled later. "I lost it [his composure], mainly because I thought of the circumstances—that it might cause a loss for those other eleven guys who worked so hard."

When Fred Couples dumped a nine-iron shot into the

water and bogeyed the final hole at the 1989 Ryder Cup, allowing the Europeans to retain the Cup, the golfer wept.

"I really took the defeat probably too hard," he recalled. "I was a good golfer and I deserved to be on the team. If I could have won my match, then we would have won the Ryder Cup. But because I lost on the last hole, we tied and they got to keep the Cup.

"Any other time I lose a tournament, it's real disappointing until I get out of the locker room and get in a car and drive somewhere. But at this Ryder Cup, I couldn't get it out of my mind. I'm not afraid to say I cried.

"Here I am, a young kid, and I've never played in anything like that. All I saw was Ray Floyd and Tom Watson and Curtis Strange and Lanny Wadkins—there're four guys who have won all these major championships and won Ryder Cups and busted their butts the whole time—and here I am. I could have won a match and helped win the Ryder Cup. And that hurt. To be on the team and win with those guys would have been the ultimate. So, just looking at them, I broke down."

Couples said that Floyd offered consolation and then told him, "This will make you a better player."

Floyd was right. "I felt like it was an experience that made me tougher in competition," said Couples.

In the 1991 Ryder Cup, which the United States won, Couples was paired with Floyd, who encouraged his partner to show the killer instinct: "Don't tell 'em 'Nice shot' all the time. Be friendly, but don't say 'Great going' all the time. We're trying to beat these guys for one week. You can be friendly with them another time."

Hale Irwin, who was involved in one of the most intense Ryder Cup matches in the event's history in 1991, watched hardly any of the 1993 matches on TV—because it was too nerve-racking.

Irwin played the final singles in 1991 and tied Bernhard Langer, preserving the Cup for the Americans.

"I just couldn't turn on the television this time," he said. "I watched about five minutes, but my stomach started churning and I had to turn the TV off. It was just too emotional for me. That day [in 1991] was the most pressure I have ever felt in my twenty-five years as a pro. In 1993, it was just too close to '91, so I couldn't watch."

Peter Jacobsen was playing in the B.C. Open during Ryder Cup week and admitted that watching the event on television during breaks hurt him on the course.

"The TV was on in the locker room and everyone was watching it instead of going out to hit balls," Jacobsen recalled. "On Sunday I had started out real well on the course and then we had a rain delay, so everyone came in and gathered around the television.

"We got word that the round would resume in thirty minutes and normally I would get right outside and start loosening up. But I was watching Davis Love's match against Costantino Rocca and I kept saying, 'I'll just watch one more shot.' Then, 'I'll just watch one more shot.' It was so exciting I just couldn't tear myself away. Finally, I got out of there just in time to run up to the tee and start playing. But it cost me. I went bogey-bogey my first two holes.

"It was amazing what was happening in that locker room. All the guys were hollering and cheering when our guys hit a good shot."

■

Rocco Mediate, who finished fifteenth on the Ryder Cup points list and failed to make the team, was determined that somehow, some way he would participate in the 1991 event. So the pro signed on as a photographer's helper and lugged camera equipment for three days over the seaside South Carolina course at Kiawah Island.

Pass the Pigs

Payne Stewart and Paul Azinger managed to keep their fellow teammates loose during the 1993 Ryder Cup at the Belfry in Sutton Coldfield, England.

At the team room in the evenings, the duo played a game called "Pass the Pigs," which featured tiny rubber pigs that were thrown like dice. Scoring depended on how the pigs landed. None of the other players seemed to understand how to play it, but, said teammate Chip Beck, "whatever it was, those two certainly played it with a lot of enthusiasm."

So much so that "Pass the Pigs" became the Americans' rallying cry as they whipped the Europeans, 15–13.

■

Team spirit—an emotion not felt on the PGA Tour—surges through the veins of the Ryder Cup players.

"I have never felt anything quite like what I felt when Chip and I were finishing our Ryder Cup match," recalled John Cook. "Most of the guys were finished with their matches and had come out onto the course to cheer us on. They were yelling, screaming, and thrusting their fists in the air. There's something about having a Lanny Wadkins cheering you on that is really special. I will never, ever forget that moment."

There's a big difference between playing in a major and in the Ryder Cup, says Corey Pavin. "In the Ryder Cup, when you're not playing a match, you're walking along the course, watching the other matches with your teammates. Everybody feels the exact same thing. And that's rare in golf. On tour, the only people who feel the same as you are your family members."

Ryder Cup teammates try to help each other relax on the course, he said. In his first match in the 1993 event, Pavin was lining up a long birdie putt on the 13th hole. Playing partner Lanny Wadkins walked up to him and said flip-pantly, "I've made that putt."

"Well, if *you* can make it, *I* certainly can," Pavin replied. And then he drained it. Together, he and Wadkins defeated Mark James and Sam Torrance, 4 and 3.

Pavin's burning desire to win inspired his Ryder Cup teammates.

"I just try to get in a mental match play attitude, which is 'go kill them,'" said Pavin. "You can really hurt an opponent if you do things that surprise him. And for me, it's enjoyable to do that, to scratch out a par or hole out from nowhere. That's very demoralizing in match play."

**"I was so nervous,
I felt like changing my underpants."**

— Confession of Europe's
Ryder Cup rookie Peter Baker
after his first match in 1993
when he and Ian Woosnam beat
the Americans one up

Hacking Their Way to Victory

During the opening match of the 1991 Ryder Cup, Seve Ballesteros and Jose Maria Olazabal teamed up against Chip Beck and Paul Azinger. The Americans were 3 up at the nine-hole turn, but the Spaniards won five of the next eight holes to close out the Yanks after the 17th.

Azinger blamed the loss on a distracting habit of Balles-teros's—a constant clearing of his throat whenever the

Americans were about to hit. "Believe me, guys, he [Balles-teros] is the king of gamesmanship," Azinger told the press after the match. "He knows every trick in the book."

The Spaniard scoffed at the charge, claiming he had a bad cold. But the Americans knew better. Looking back at the incident, Beck says, "the most disappointing thing was to learn that a truly gifted player like Seve could be capable of behavior that I thought was unsportsmanlike. It really threw me for a loop."

How Does "Sven" Ballesteros Sound?

When the United States team held onto the Cup in 1993, European fans were not happy—especially with the play of Spaniard Seve Ballesteros.

A joke making the rounds in Britain after the Europeans lost went like this: "Did you know that there were two Scandinavians on the European team? Joakim Haeggman, who is Swedish, and Seve Ballesteros, who is Finished."

Life on the Tour

On a scale of 1 to 10 (terrible to great), how glamorous is the Tour?

David Feherty: "It's a 5. It probably seems glamorous when you watch a guy with a four-shot lead win a quarter of a million dollars, but it is pretty short-lived."

Andrew Magee: "I'd give it a 7.5. Sometimes it is very glamorous out here, but quite often it's the complete opposite."

Bill Glasson: "It can wear on you, but I wouldn't want to do anything else, so I'd have to give it a 10. After all, it's the greatest job in the world."

Scott Simpson: "A 7. We do go to beautiful places, but we do our own laundry, don't always stay in the nicest places, and we have to travel."

Jim McGovern: "It's a 4. Living in a suitcase, a different bed every week. It wears you out."

Mark Calcavecchia: "About a 5. It's only glamorous for the guys who win. If you're struggling, not making cuts, it is no place to be."

Payne Stewart: "It's a 9. It's fun. We work for ourselves, get to be outdoors, go to the nicest places. The drawback is time away from our families."

What's the biggest myth about the Tour?

Billy Andrade: "That you have to be a perfect golfer, that you have to hit every shot perfect or be some kind of robot, hit every green, make all the putts. You don't have to be great in every aspect of the game."

Craig Stadler: "That we lead the so-called 'star's life.' It's not the easiest job in the world. There's not much family life out here, not much glamour."

John Cook: "That we're all faceless clones."

Jesper Parnevik: "That it is hard to make friends with the players here. You hear that they treat golf as purely business and aren't very friendly. But that hasn't been the case."

Jim Gallagher Jr.: "People think the guys who don't make it out here aren't good. But there is such a small difference between great and good. There are as many good players who don't make it out here as do."

Lee Janzen: "That the guys on top are so much different than the guys around seventieth place. The only real difference is the guys at the top know they are going to play well and the guys around seventieth just hope they will."

Having a Ball

Celebrating a major championship can be as much fun as winning it.

Hours after the end of the 1986 British Open, a security guard noticed a party under the moonlight on the 18th green of Turnberry's Ailsa Course. Upon investigating further, the guard found Greg Norman—who'd won the championship there earlier that day—with a group of friends toasting his victory. The guard allowed the party to continue.

Celebrating a major championship in grand style may be a lost art, though, because of the increased demands on today's champions. The first hour or two after a victory is filled with press interviews, then the player often has to catch a flight to the next tournament. Norman, after his second British Open win in 1993, was on his jet headed back to America within a couple of hours of the award ceremony. No 18th-green party this time.

If the winner stays in town, it's usually for a quick dinner with family, a few hours' sleep, maybe an early-morning appearance on "Good Morning America," then on to the next event.

He might have a chance for an impromptu party—or maybe not. After Jose Maria Olazabal's 1994 Masters victory, his manager, Sergio Gomez, went to a convenience store and grabbed all the champagne he could find. When he got to the counter, he was informed that alcohol isn't sold on Sunday in Augusta, Georgia.

Some of Tom Watson's most treasured memories are the hours spent after the 1977 British Open at Turnberry, where he bested Jack Nicklaus. That evening, Watson and his wife Linda were in their hotel room, which overlooked the course. "It was warm and the sun was shining into the room," Watson recalled. "All the people were gone from the golf course, but the stands and scoreboard were there. At about nine o'clock, a lone Scottish bagpiper came along and played his pipes for close to an hour. It gave me chills and indelibly printed on my memory the whole championship—what it was all about, winning in Scotland against Jack Nicklaus. I think it was then that I really fell in love with the game."

After he won at Muirfield in 1980, Watson impetuously played a two-hole match for fun with fellow competitor Ben Crenshaw in the Scottish twilight.

"It was right after dinner, about 9:30, and still light out," said Watson. "We'd had champagne and as I was walking back to the room after dinner, I saw Ben and a bunch of people out near the 18th green. They said they were going to watch Ben play 10 and 18 with some old clubs and a gutta-percha ball, so I said, 'Come on, Crenshaw, we'll play 10 and 18 for the British Open.'" Watson won for the second time that day (although he used a modern ball against Crenshaw's ancient "guttie").

When Lanny Wadkins won the 1977 PGA Championship at Pebble Beach, he partied so hard it almost cost him his entire winnings. After sharing a couple bottles of the bubbly with his wife, Wadkins fell asleep in his hotel room. At about three A.M., Wadkins woke up, and as he walked by the fireplace, he came across a crumpled piece of paper. "I picked it up and it was my winner's check for $45,000," Wadkins recalled. "I had balled it up and thrown it at the fireplace at some point."

Jerry Pate didn't toss away that much money after he won the U.S. Open in 1976, but he can't say how many thousands he lost to country singers Roy Clark and Charley Pride. Hours after his victory in Atlanta, he flew to Iowa for a pro-am the next day. Shortly after landing, he met Clark and Pride, who were also slated to play in the pro-am. He ended up playing poker with them until four in the morning.

"We were playing a hundred-dollar minimum, and I didn't even know how to sort the cards," Pate recalled. "I didn't know much about poker and they did. They asked, 'Are you sure you want to play for this much money?' I said, 'I don't care. I just won the U.S. Open.' I lost so much I couldn't count it."

The thrill of winning a major lingers through the first night and on into the next day.

"When I won my first U.S. Open in 1988, I was so excited I couldn't sleep," recalled Curtis Strange. Feeling he had to talk to someone, Strange phoned his twin brother Allan, at four A.M., apologizing for calling in the middle of the night. "That's all right," said Allan. "I can't sleep either."

Ben Crenshaw said that he was overcome with emotion the night of his 1984 Masters victory. When he arrived at the Augusta home he was using during the tournament, his housemates, the country-singing Gatlin Brothers, greeted him by standing on their heads. He declined their invitation to party. Instead, he downed two stiff Scotches and headed for bed. But he was still too excited to sleep.

"I went back out to Augusta National and walked around the course the next morning, then I went home to Austin and ate Mexican food as soon as I could," Crenshaw said. "Later, I got a videotape of the tournament and watched it—and I cried for about four days."

Larry Mize was so keyed up the day after he won the Masters in 1987 that he let loose with a scream at the top of his lungs while driving from Augusta to Hilton Head Island, South Carolina, for the following week's MCI Heritage Classic.

Bernhard Langer, on the other hand, just wanted to walk the empty Augusta fairways after his first Masters win in 1985. He and his wife Vikki walked hand-in-hand down Washington Road, but arrived at the course too early and found the gates shut. Langer had to be content with peeking through the chain-link fence, taking in the same view of Augusta National available to the eyes of curious nonmembers.

It only proves that sooner or later life returns to normal for the champion. It didn't take long for Sandy Lyle to be humbled after winning the 1985 British Open.

The following afternoon, at a victory party held at his home in Wentworth, England, he ran out of food. So, with Nick Faldo in the passenger side, Lyle drove down the road and returned with several cartons from a Chinese takeout.

After dinner, the British Open champion was spotted in the kitchen, wrapping up the celebration of his first major championship by washing the dishes.

> *"I think it was Confucius who said,*
> *'If you find a job you like,*
> *you'll never work a day the rest*
> *of your life.' Golf has never*
> *been work for me.*
> *You don't work golf. You play it."*
>
> —Tom Kite

Aside from the travel and separation from the family, what is the toughest thing about playing golf for a living?

Lanny Wadkins: "Discipline when it comes to practicing, staying in shape, and eating right. We don't have a coach out here. You've got to do it all yourself."

Fuzzy Zoeller: "Laundry. I'm not a very good ironer."

Wayne Levi: "The hardest thing is to motivate myself to practice as much as I used to. Once I get out there, I'll practice for two or three hours. I still love to practice more than play."

Ian Baker-Finch: "The mental side. It's very tough on the mind competing out here, keeping mental stability. There are so many ups and downs, and you have to realize that there'll be more downs than ups."

On the Road Again

When Brad Bryant joined the Tour in 1978, he chose to travel in a pickup truck and haul a trailer home.

"I had more fun doing that than anything I've ever done on tour," he said. "I traveled with about five fishing rods and two tackle boxes and a shotgun and a guitar. It was great. You could practice real hard and work on your game. Then when I walked in the door of the mobile home, it was like going home. Instead of walking into a motel room, I was actually home.

"It was a lot easier lifestyle back then. We were qualifying on Monday, trying like the devil to make the cut on Friday. But the thing was, if you didn't qualify on Monday, you went fishing for a couple of days."

But now times are different. The Tour is so spread out that Bryant flies from one place to another. "There are trade-offs in everything," he said. "The Tour has become a bigger business and you can make a lot more money. But it's a lot less fun than when I first started."

■

The average Tour player spends between $100,000 and $150,000 a year in travel expenses.

Men of Letters

What do the letters in pro golfer JC Andersen's first name stand for?

Absolutely nothing. It's his given name, with no periods. Even though he was born a few minutes past Christmas, he says JC isn't derived from Jesus Christ. His moniker was inspired by his parents' names. His mother's maiden name begins with a J and his father's middle initial is C.

■

D.A. Weibring is often asked, "What's the D.A. stand for?" His reply: "Don't Ask." (For the record, it's Donald Albert.)

**Who has the strongest arms
on the Tour?**

Jim Thorpe
Fulton Allem
Keith Clearwater
Greg Norman
Greg Twiggs
Ed Dougherty
Andy Bean

If there was a "Jeopardy!" contest on tour, who would win?

Ken Green: "Let's see, who is the most intelligent creature out here? To be honest, I don't think we have any brains on tour."

Dan Forsman: "I can't think of anyone out here who is a real scholar although Kirk Triplett would probably do well."

John Cook: "Maybe nobody. Curt Byrum might win. He's a 'Jeopardy!' maniac and he could answer the questions."

Dave Stockton Jr.: "Tom Kite or Tom Watson. They're both very knowledgeable people."

Scott Hoch: "Mike Donald. When it comes to stats, sports, and other trivia, he knows quite a bit."

David Frost: "It might be tough for some of us. But I'd probably go with Fulton Allem. He knows everything."

Mike Reid: "Ed Sneed. He's just an intelligent individual. Chess is one of his hobbies, so he must have something between the ears."

What kind of books do you read?

Ken Green: "Reading is not a big hobby of mine. Occasionally, I try to read a book that could improve my mind—but it never works."

John Cook: "I read a variety of authors from John Grisham to Rush Limbaugh."

Dave Stockton Jr.: "John Grisham books."

Dan Forsman: "Books on current events, self-help, psychology, parenting, health, and religion."

Scott Hoch: "I read a lot of magazines and newspapers. But I can't sit down and read a book. I did enough of that in school."

David Frost: "I like autobiographies—Churchill, Nixon, Muhammad Ali. I also like detective fiction. I read a lot."

Mike Reid: "I read quite a bit. I like biographies, historical novels, and old golf books."

Playing for Fun

Can golf ever be just a game again for the pros? Can they still have fun playing with their friends? Can they get enjoyment out of playing for five dollars a hole when a week earlier they were shooting for a $100,000 prize?

Away from the Tour, most pros still make time to play with old golfing buddies. "I play all the time when I'm back home," says Steve Pate. "It's a lot more fun than playing on the Tour."

However, there are some pros who say that they don't have time to play for fun. "There are so many other things in your life," said Jeff Sluman. "You've got to take care of things when you're home. Besides, if you take three or four weeks off and truly get away from the golf course, then you can come back fresher and stronger. So I have just about stopped playing golf for fun."

But many others simply can't resist the lure of the links.

Andrew Magee loves the little two-dollar bets with friends at the Phoenix Country Club. "I play almost every day when I'm home," he said. "It doesn't have to be for big money to be fun."

Paul Azinger says he likes playing with club members at the River Wilderness Country Club in Bradenton, Florida. Bizarre bets and fines add to the enjoyment of golf. For example, when a playing partner farts, everyone must pay the wind-breaker a dollar.

Fulton Allen worries that he plays too much golf in his free time. Allem lives on the course at Heathrow Country Club in suburban Orlando and plays every day that he's in town. "I go hang out with my pals and we beat the ball around every morning," he said. "I don't rest when I'm home—and that's something I should be doing."

In contrast, Mark McCumber thinks that he doesn't play enough when he's home at Ponte Vedre Beach, Florida. "Years ago, I played golf all the time," he said. "Then I began thinking, 'This is my business. I shouldn't be doing this when I'm home.' Well, that's kind of a bad attitude. Golf, after all, is still a game. We just happen to make a living at it. We tend to forget sometimes how this game made us laugh and how much pleasure it brought us when we were young."

Raymond Floyd hasn't forgotten. When he goes home to Miami, he golfs with his sons, twenty-year-old Raymond Jr. and eighteen-year-old Robert. "They're pretty good," he said. "If they start playing really well, I start needling them. You know it works—the old man can still psyche them out."

Is it still just a game? It certainly is fun for the greatest recreational golfer in American history.

When Arnold Palmer comes home to Bay Hill in Orlando, he plays in the member shoot-outs three times a week. "I play with everybody," he says. "Guys show up and you might get matched up with a high-handicapper as well as a low-handicapper. You get your group, you go to the first tee, and start swinging. I love that kind of golf. That is the essence of the sport—just going out and playing. It's fun. It's enjoyable. In fact, that's about as enjoyable as life can get."

What do you do to relax off the course?

Paul Azinger: "My true love is saltwater fishing. I'm totally into it. Fishing is my escape mechanism."

Fred Couples: "I love to relax in front of the TV. That's it. I'll watch just about anything. It doesn't matter that much what it is. I especially like some of the old reruns. Some nights I'll watch TV from seven to eleven. I've turned into a zombie. I hate to go out."

Payne Stewart: "I love pro basketball and have season tickets to the Orlando Magic home games. I'm always screaming at the officials—especially the three-second violations which they seldom call. I lose my voice by halftime. [His wife] Tracey won't sit by me."

For relaxation, Stewart spends hours fishing from one of his two boats. Cooking is another one of his passions. "I've got this special marinade I make with ingredients that no one else knows. I'll give it to [his daughter] Chelsea when she's old enough to leave the house. But not until then."

Davis Love III: "I'm an avid hunter and fisherman. When I go hunting, it's the best time in the world for me. I can sit up in a tree for four or five hours. Nobody bothers me."

John Daly: "I enjoy playing the guitar to occupy my free time. Larry Rinker got me interested in plucking out tunes. Ever since I picked up the guitar, it's helped me a lot. I'll sit there and make the dogs bark, but I lose track of time because I enjoy it so much. I'm terrible, but it keeps my mind occupied."

Nick Price: "It's a huge contrast for me when I finish up on a Sunday under intense pressure, with thousands of people watching, and the next afternoon, I'm out on my boat in a lake. It's a total unwind. That's why so many golfers like to fish."

David Edwards: "Flying. I like things that make noise and go fast."

Bobby Clampett: "Flying allows you to focus on something other than golf, but yet uses many of the same attributes."

Bruce Lietzke: "I've never won a major championship, but I bet Jack Nicklaus hasn't had one of his cars featured in a car magazine like I have."

Tom Purtzer: "I love horses. My ideal for relaxing is to spend time with my family and my horses. I love to get away from the rat race."

Peter Jacobsen: "I collect muscle cars and play music."

■

Among other golfers' hobbies:

Fulton Allem: riding and breeding horses

Mark Brooks: cooking

Ben Crenshaw: birdwatching and collecting golf artifacts

Ed Dougherty: caring for one of the finest Lionel train collections in North America

Steve Elkington: drawing faces

Lee Janzen: music, movies, and quoting dialogue from the TV sitcom "Seinfeld"

Tom Kite: landscaping

Nick Price: building model airplanes, shooting a bow and arrow, and tinkering with his golf clubs

Nick Faldo: trout fishing and flying helicopters

Bruce Lietzke: fishing and driving a fleet of seven race cars for pleasure

There's No Place Like Home

Although some golfers bring their families with them on tour, they'd prefer to spend more time with the wife and kids at home.

"The worst thing about being a professional golfer is the time you're away from home," says Bruce Lietzke. But unlike most of the Tour pros, he does something about it. He simply plays fewer tournaments so he can spend more time with his family—wife Rosemarie, son Stephen, ten, and daughter Christine, eight, at their home in Dallas. He enjoys coaching kids' softball and soccer.

Lietzke, forty-three, and now in his twentieth season on the PGA Tour, has won twelve titles and nearly five million dollars.

But in 1994, he missed such tournaments as the U.S. Open and the British Open. "Years ago, guys told me that I was wasting my talent," said Lietzke. "Now those same guys come up and say, 'I understand.' Maybe they have kids now or are married or are easing into midlife.

"There are still a few guys who ask me, 'What's the real reason you won't play in the U.S. Open?' It's really because my son has Little League. My family life is more important than any golf tournament."

Gene Sauers has found himself torn between trying to be a family man and being a top pro golfer.

In his first nine years on the Tour, starting in 1984, the Georgia native increased his earnings each year and placed among the top forty money winners for seven straight years.

But after he got married in 1988 and started to raise a family, the father of three young boys began getting home-sick. "I miss the hell out of my family," admitted the two-time winner. "It's so hard now. It's gradually gotten harder because it drives me crazy not being able to watch my kids grow up."

At the end of 1993, his earnings had plunged from a career-high $434,566 (32nd on the money list) in 1992 to $117,608 (128th on the list).

"Occasionally, the family joins me on tour. But that's tough on all of us as well. When they're around, I want to spend time with them and it disrupts my schedule. Damned if you do and damned if you don't."

Nick Price says he became a world-class golfer only after he worked on his swing—and became a family man.

He credits the birth of his first child, Gregory, in 1991 with making a big change for the better in his life—both on and off the course.

"I didn't marry until I was thirty," Price said, "and we didn't have our first child until I was thirty-four. That has been a real settling influence on me.

"Before, golf was my entire life, my everything. But when my son was born, I discovered something else. Ever since then, I don't get bent out of shape when I have a bad round. There's something else to live for, something else to come home to. I've got a wife, a son, and a daughter and they are so much more important to me than golf.

"Now I don't feel all that pressure. My life is going to be happy regardless of what I do on the course. I've changed my priorities and it's made a big difference.

"If being number one comes, great. But if it doesn't, I'm still a very happy man."

But as his golf fortunes soar, so do the demands on his time. After winning the 1992 PGA Championship, Price spent forty nights at home in 1993, compared to eighty in 1992. He also was besieged with twice the number of interview requests per week, from ten to twenty during major championships.

Brad Faxon often brings his family on tour with him. He says he's never so serious about golf that he can't go back to the hotel room and forget about what's happened that day on the course.

Waiting will be his wife Bonnie and two daughters, Melanie, five, and Emily, three. For some, young children would be a distraction. For Faxon, they are a godsend.

"They've never been a handicap to me," he said. "They don't care what you shot. All they know is that you're Daddy and you're home and it's time to play.

"On the golf course, everyone is a little bit on the too-serious side. With kids, it helps to take the pressures off when you finish a round. I don't like to carry those pressures with me."

John Cook said he used to come home from the Tour and be obsessed with fixing his game. "But now when I'm home from the Tour, I spend almost all my time with my family. That way, I return refreshed and ready to concentrate on my game."

Cook—a family man with kids ages thirteen, ten, and eight—says he tries to take each child on an individual trip with him on the Tour each year.

■

Most of the dozen competitors in the 1994 Royal Caribbean Classic who lived within a two- or three-hour drive from the Miami event stayed in nearby hotels to save themselves the stress of the commute.

But not Lee Trevino. Not when he had a chance to see his two kids—one-year-old Lee Daniel and five-year-old Olivia—at his Jupiter Island home every day. Trevino made the five-hour round-trip drive every day.

"When I could put my son to bed every night and wake him up and give him breakfast every morning, that made the trip worthwhile for me," said Trevino.

The commute didn't hurt his golf game in the least. He won the tournament in a playoff and pocketed $120,000.

A Wife's Life on the Tour

It's far from a glamorous life for the wife of a PGA Tour pro, says Kelli Maggert, wife of Jeff Maggert.

"Life on the Tour is rarely glamorous," she said. "It's really just like having a regular nine-to-five job. We go to dinner, play with the kids, and go to bed."

Kelli, who wed the golfer in 1988, said the first years of their marriage were lean ones. Jeff failed to get his PGA Tour card, so he traveled the Australian and Asian tours.

The couple planned to have a family, but only after Jeff was playing well and bringing in enough money. At the time, he was doing neither. Their only source of income was from Kelli's job as an English teacher.

But while in India in 1988, Kelli got pregnant. "It couldn't have come at a worse time, financially," she said.

"But there was nothing else to do in Calcutta—no Johnny Carson to watch on TV at night."

A few weeks after Matt was born in December of 1988, Jeff returned to the Asian tour, leaving Kelli with almost no money. "We had eighty-five dollars to our name—that's it—after the expenses of Christmas, a new baby, and hospital bills," she recalled. "And I was still on unpaid pregnancy leave from my teaching job, so we had no way to get money.

"Jeff promised that as soon as he made any money, he would wire it home. But I had to take Matt to the doctor that day. He handed me a bill for $365, payable on demand. I told him I forgot my checkbook and gave him the eighty-five dollars I had in my purse."

Meanwhile, Jeff played in an Asian tournament that week under more pressure than he had ever felt. Fortunately, he played his best ever up to then, winning $20,000. "To us," said Kelli, "it was like a million."

But, she added, "We only got to keep two thousand dollars of that money. The rest went to Jeff's sponsors. That's how deep in the hole we were."

By the time their daughter Macy was born in 1990, Maggert had won tournaments on both the Asian and Australian tours. He also played in the United States on the Ben Hogan Tour where he was named Player of the Year with earnings of $108,644. As a PGA Tour rookie in 1991, Maggert finished second behind John Daly in first-year winnings with $240,940.

By mid-1994, Maggert had won one PGA tournament and collected more than two million dollars in Tour winnings.

"Life certainly has improved for us," said Kelli. "We look back at those early days and laugh.

"Things are so nice now. Maybe I take it for granted a little bit, but I really appreciate how lucky we are. It blows my mind that we can just buy a car, not worrying about financing it—that's not a little thing."

The Maggerts travel with their children, who spend part of the time in day-care facilities provided by the tournaments.

"I was talking to Barbara Nicklaus at the U.S. Open, saying how great the day-care was there, and she just looked at me and said, 'You don't know how lucky you are. We didn't have such things when I was raising the kids.' I can't imagine how they used to do it years ago."

Nowadays, almost every tournament has a nursery for the players' children. That way, she said, she can follow her husband on the course.

Ironically, the one tournament that Maggert won—the 1993 Walt Disney World/Oldsmobile Classic—didn't have day-care, so Kelli didn't get to watch her husband play a single hole except the last one on the final day.

When Maggert sank the putt to win the tournament, Kelli was calm, having learned from the example of her low-key husband not to get churned up over every birdie or bogey.

"The first year on the Tour, I got so excited, I couldn't eat or sleep," she said. "But after a few times like that, you learn to keep your nerves in check. But I still feel for him.

"I want to throw a club for him, or kick his bag for him since he won't do it—just to make him feel better."

Unlike some other golf marriages, the emotional life of the family doesn't revolve around the success or failures of the golfer's game. "Jeff is such an even-keel person, he never comes home mad from the golf course," Kelli said. "He's kind of a dream husband—for a golfer."

Till Double Bogeys Do Us Part

Pro golfer Billy Mayfair and his longtime girlfriend Tammy McIntire were married in 1994 near the 18th green of the Four Seasons/Tournament Players Course in Las Colinas, Texas. "We're going to be spending the rest of our lives on a golf course," Mayfair said. "We thought we might as well be married on one."

■

In 1993, rookie tour pro Bob Friend planned to ask his girlfriend Leslie Minard to marry him by having his proposal posted on the tournament leader board at the Federal Express St. Jude Classic.

But CBS sports announcer Jim Nantz had a better idea.

He had Friend pop the question during the taping of an interview that would later be shown on the golf broadcast. Then, Friend invited Leslie to the CBS production facility, ostensibly to preview the interview.

To Leslie, it looked like a nice piece about her sweetheart—that is, until the end of the interview. On the tape, Friend turned to the camera and said, "I love you very much, Leslie. Will you marry me?"

In the production facility, the stunned Leslie turned to Friend and said, "Yes!"

■

Tammie Green credits her victory in the 1993 Health-South Classic to her nuptials. That win gave her enough in earnings to get a marriage proposal.

Later that year she wed *Golfweek* magazine editor Steve Ellis after a long courtship. "Steve said he'd marry me when I made my first million," she said.

Wife, Mother . . . Golf Instructor?

Some wives on the PGA Tour take their husband's golf so seriously they sound like instructors.

When Payne Stewart's wife Tracey arrived after the second round of the 1993 Players Championship at the TPC at Sawgrass, she greeted her husband by pointing out a flaw in his putting stroke.

Recalled Stewart, "The first thing she says to me is 'I saw you on TV and you're decelerating with your putter.' Not 'Hi, honey, how are you doing?' or anything like that."

Stewart obviously paid attention to Tracey. He went out the next morning and shot a 66—the best round of the day—although he blew up to a 74 in the final round to finish in a tie for eleventh.

Priceless Mementos

When Nick Price was gunning for the 1992 PGA Championship at Bellerive, his good friend Don Bryant said he would break out a special bottle of wine should Price win.

When Price won, Bryant brought a 1961 magnum of Petrus—a French Bordeaux worth a few thousand dollars—to Price's small victory party. Price and his wife Sue drank from it, as did his caddie Jeff "Squeeky" Medlen, his golf guru David Leadbetter, and the Bryants.

Today that empty magnum sits in the Prices' home, accorded its place along with the trophies. On the bottle are the signatures of the friends who attended the victory celebration.

■

In one of golf's most dramatic moments, Paul Azinger holed out from a bunker on the 18th hole to capture the 1993 Memorial at Muirfield Village Golf Club.

A bucket of sand from that very bunker sits in the home of Azinger's proud parents in Sarasota, Florida, courtesy of the folks at Muirfield Village.

The Seniors

Are the Seniors better today than they were when they played on the PGA Tour?

The courses on the Senior PGA Tour are shorter and in better condition than when the golfers played on the regular Tour years ago. Also, the pins are more accessible today, all factors that help lower scores. But even without those benefits, most seniors say they've improved with age.

Bob Murphy: "Certain areas of my game are better than they ever were. Driving, for instance. I trust that I'm going to bust it down the middle."

Compared to his stats from 1986—his most lucrative year on the PGA Tour—Murphy's drives in 1993 averaged eight yards farther, his driving accuracy increased from 70 to 73 percent, his percentage of greens in regulation shot up from 62 to 74, and he shaved two points off his average score, from 72.2 down to 70.2.

Jim Colbert: "I'm more accurate off the tee and more consistent with my putting."

Compared to his best year on the PGA Tour, which was 1983, his driving accuracy has increased from 63 to 75 percent, the percentage of greens in regulation has jumped from 63 to 70, and he's whittled nearly one stroke off his average to 70.6.

Lee Trevino: "I know more about the game. Also, I have more time now to practice and that's the thing I like to do the most. I hit golf balls each and every day. If I'm not better, I'm at least as good as I was in 1980."

Compared to his best year on the PGA Tour in 1980, Trevino has increased his driving distance from 259.2 yards to 265.6, maintained the exact same driving accuracy at 72 percent, upped the percentage of greens in regulation from 70 to 74, and has virtually the same stroke average of 70.

Mike Hill: "I'm looser and I strike the ball better. I'm also not as volatile as I once was."

Gibby Gilbert: "The difference today is more maturity. It took me fifty years to figure that out. I used to be very hard on myself. I still get aggravated with myself every once in a while, but basically I can accept the bad shots with the good."

Rocky Thompson: "I'm way better than I was back then. If I could have driven the ball then the way I do now, I'd have won a lot more."

Older but Wiser

Although the courses are shorter, greens are slower, and the lifestyle is easier than on the regular PGA Tour, the Senior PGA Tour is tougher than you think.

Just ask Raymond Floyd.

"I honestly didn't think it would be as competitive as it is," said Floyd, who won three times in his first year on the Senior Tour in 1992. (He was the first golfer to win on both the PGA and Senior PGA Tour in the same year.)

"I was absolutely astounded by some of the guys whom I hadn't seen in years. They were 50 percent better players.

"Let's be honest. They left because they weren't competitive. They left because they couldn't cut it anymore. They decided to pursue something else. Now, all of a sudden, they're competing against each other and it's phenomenal. I see guys who are longer off the tee, straighter off the tee, and have better short games than they ever had on the regular Tour."

Floyd's arrival on the Senior PGA Tour caused some friction among the players because he wondered publicly if the Tour would be too easy for him.

"We laughed," said Jim Albus, winner of the 1993 GTE Suncoast Classic. "Raymond made comments before he came out. He really thought he was going to win every event. He was that confident. In fact, he made one comment that made a lot of guys mad. He was going to play the regular Tour because he thought it was unfair for him to play the Senior PGA Tour.

"That got a lot of guys rankled, and a lot of eyebrows up. Raymond is a great player. But I think it's harder for him than he thought. He's not having the picnic he thought it was going to be."

Lee Trevino, who has won eighteen times on the Senior PGA Tour since he joined it in 1989, admits he underestimated the skill of the players.

"The talent was a hell of a lot better than I thought," he said. "I saw the scores they were shooting and said, 'How are these guys doing it?' Then I went out and saw for myself. I spent a lot of time preparing for the seniors out of fear—fear of failure."

Added Arnold Palmer, "The competition has gotten more and more fierce. And it will continue that way as the young guys come to play."

You're Dog Meat, Rookie

When Lee Trevino joined the Senior PGA Tour in 1989, he was quoted in the papers as saying, "I expect to win five tournaments or more the first year." (It was a statement he later denied making.)

The bold quote raised the hackles of many seniors.

So when Trevino made his Senior PGA Tour debut at Royal Kaanapali, Hawaii, he opened his locker and, on the top shelf, found a surprise—a can of dog food with his name inscribed on it.

"We decided to give him the breakfast of rookies," said Larry Ziegler. "One thing you have to understand about the dog food joke. We only did it because we know Lee can take it."

(For the record, in his first full year on the Senior PGA Tour in 1990, Trevino won seven tournaments and was the first to earn over one million dollars in a single season.)

> **"They keep talking about the Big Four — Palmer, Nicklaus, Player, and Trevino. I just want to be the fifth wheel in case somebody gets a flat."**
>
> — Chi Chi Rodriguez

Then and Now

Sam Snead: "In 1939, I was the leading money winner with $19,000. Today, they get more than that for finishing fifth in one tournament."

Paul Runyan: "The first Masters [in 1934] was a fun tournament. They had fifty gallons of good corn whiskey and ran out by midmorning of the third day of the tournament. No one was inebriated, but we had fun. They may have fun today, but they don't have that good corn whiskey."

Tommy Bolt: "I know I had a reputation for throwing clubs, but there's more to it than just letting them fly. Today, I see young guys throw their clubs backward—and that's wrong. You should always throw a club ahead of you so that you don't have to walk any extra distance to get it."

Dave Hill: "Many of the greens back then were like washboards. Now it's like putting on your own private pool table."

Gary Player says there should be
a Super Senior PGA Tour
for players over the age of eighty.
"Tournaments will only be three holes,"
he says. "Whoever remembers
his score, wins."

King of Hearts

Of all the players on the Senior PGA Tour, none is considered by his peers to be more selfless off the course than Chi Chi Rodriguez.

"He'll never be as great a golfer as he is a human being," said fellow pro Bill Kratzert. Chi Chi's mantle is lined with humanitarian awards, including the 1986 Card Walker Award from the PGA Tour for outstanding contributions to Junior Golf, the 1987 National Puerto Rico Coalition Life Achievement Award, the 1988 Old Tom Morris Award, the

1989 Bob Jones Award—the USGA's highest honor—and the 1993 Herb Graffis Award.

Chi Chi's favorite charity is the Chi Chi Rodriguez Foundation for troubled youth, based in Clearwater, Florida. He has raised more than a million dollars for the organization, which has steered more than seven hundred disadvantaged kids into productive lives.

"It's hard for a kid to steal your hubcaps when he's carrying your golf bag," said Chi Chi. "When you give to kids, you get back twice as much. These kids have been defeated all their lives. We are showing them they can succeed. I love to help young people because I was never a kid myself. I was too poor to be a child, so I never really had a childhood."

Born the fifth of six children near San Juan, Puerto Rico, Chi Chi was working alongside his father in the sugarcane fields by the time he was six years old.

"My dad worked fourteen hours a day every day of his life," Chi Chi recalled. "He never made more than eighteen dollars a week. He would come home dead-tired and hungry. But if he saw a kid with a big belly—the sign of malnutrition—he would give him his rice and beans.

"I never forgot that. My mother always said if I was a woman, I'd always be pregnant because I don't know how to say no. But if you're not good to kids, you're not a good person. My philosophy is simple. The only thing you can take with you is what you leave behind.

"Winning tournaments does something for my ego. But seeing those kids [at his foundation] grow up and be successful means more to my heart. Sometimes I'm so tired when I get there, I want to lie down. But then somebody will say, 'The kids are waiting.' When I get to them, it's like the fountain of youth."

Gary Player the Conglomerate

Like so many pro golfers, Gary Player has branched out into a variety of business ventures.

Along with making a good living on the Senior PGA Tour, Player heads a multinational force that runs the following:

• Gary Player Enterprises, which licenses his name and likeness worldwide;

• Gary Player Design Company, which constructs golf courses;

• Gary Player Golf Academy;

• Gary Player Development Company, which handles real estate dealings;

• Gary Player Management Services, which provides turnkey club management;

• Gary Player Travel and Tours;

• Gary Player Stud, which deals in breeding thorough-breds in South Africa and Kentucky;

• Anvil Golf Company, Player's latest venture, which makes golf equipment.

Why all the businesses when the fifty-nine-year-old pro has made over three million dollars in winnings on the Senior PGA Tour? His business ventures give him the chance to compete even when he's not on the course.

"I'm a natural competitor," Player explained. "All my life I've had to compete. That's been my mark, hasn't it? Arnold [Palmer], Jack [Nicklaus], and I play against each other all the time because it's in our blood. What are we going to do when we quit playing? We all want to keep competing because it helps keep us young."

> **"I can't point that far."**
>
> — Senior Tour player Gay Brewer,
> after watching John Daly send
> a ball over a sixty-five-foot-high
> net 285 yards away on Augusta
> National's practice range

Rock(y) 'n' Roll

Senior PGA player Rocky Thompson built a long-shafted putter, painted it gold, and named it Elvis.

"I just figured gold and Elvis go together," he explained. "I also wanted it to be hungry. Elvis was always eating—he was my kind of guy."

Among other names Thompson has given his clubs are: Darryl, Son of Darryl, Linda Ronstadt, and Cherry Pie.

Grab Bag

How much time do you take to warm up before a round?

Fuzzy Zoeller: "Every day is different, depending on how I feel. Sometimes it's just five minutes, and sometimes fifteen to twenty minutes."

Greg Norman: "Forty-five minutes. I hit balls for twenty minutes and putt for fifteen, and all the walking back and forth and everything takes about ten to fifteen minutes."

Wayne Levi: "One hour. I putt for five or ten minutes, then hit balls for forty minutes and putt again for another ten minutes."

Ian Baker-Finch: "One hour. Forty minutes hitting and twenty minutes putting."

Lanny Wadkins: "An hour. I try not to rush when I am preparing for a tournament. That way, it helps slow me down because I have a tendency to play too fast out on the course."

Brad Faxon: "Half an hour to forty minutes. Twenty to twenty-five minutes on the range and ten to fifteen putting. Then maybe I'll work on my short game a little."

■

Nick Price spends about fifteen hours a week on the practice tee during tournament weeks and about twelve hours a week when he's not playing. "The weeks before majors, I crank it up to about twenty to twenty-five a week," he says. "I love to practice."

Who practices the best course management?

Tom Kite
Corey Pavin
Hale Irwin
Curtis Strange
Jeff Sluman
Jack Nicklaus
Tom Watson

Practice What You Preach

Here are four golfers' thoughts about the practice range:

Howard Twitty: "The longest distance in the world is the walk between the practice tee and the first tee—and many games have been lost in between."

Tom Lehman: "The way I hit on the practice range has no bearing on how I'll play. I don't hit balls other than to get loose."

Greg Kraft: "I've had some of my best rounds when I went out on the practice range and struggled. It seems when I struggle, I get a lot more patient on the golf course and I don't get too fancy."

Phil Blackmar: "If I hit terrible shots on the range, I might play good on the course. But if I hit it good on the range, I usually play terrible on the course."

Practice? Who Needs It?

Bruce Lietzke doesn't spend as much time on the practice range as most pros do.

"I don't practice a whole lot," he said. "I just found it easier to concentrate on one thing. I've got one swing, one way to hit the ball, and I just work on that."

Fred Couples just shakes his head. "You have to think Bruce could have been one of the great players of all time if he practiced more."

Tom Kite believes that Lietzke could win more tournaments and be a better player if he would only practice more. "But the thing is Bruce is one of the most contented people I've ever seen," said Kite. "He's totally at ease, totally happy with his lifestyle and with what he has and what he has accomplished."

Lietzke often takes a month or two off to relax and spend quality time with his family. "I totally admire somebody who can do what Bruce has done and be 100 percent happy," said Kite. "I couldn't do it. It'd drive me crazy."

Lietzke can put his clubs away for weeks at a time and not touch them until it's time for another tournament.

"It's amazing," says Corey Pavin. "I don't know how he does it. He doesn't touch a club for a month, then comes out and plays great. I wish I could do that."

One time, in 1985, Lietzke finished a tourney and wasn't slated to play in another one for two months. "I had a new caddie who didn't really know me," Lietzke recalled. "He was packing up my clubs and I told him to be careful and take out the wet towel that was in my bag because I wasn't going to be using my clubs for two months. I guess he didn't believe me or he was testing me because he slipped a big ripe banana under the head cover of my driver."

Lietzke went home, put the clubs in the garage, and returned to the Tour two months later. "I unzipped the bag, opened it up, and out came the most awful, unholy smell in the world. It was a rotten banana."

What is the biggest difference in you as a golfer from the beginning of your career to now?

Curtis Strange: "I'm more comfortable in my surroundings. When you first come out, there's an intimidation factor. You're uneasy about the future and you don't know if you belong."

Bernhard Langer: "I have a lot more experience now. I'm more mature. I know myself better—my strengths and weaknesses."

Tom Watson: "I'm a better strategist. It's not just having raw talent. I've learned how to use that talent to score."

Hal Sutton: "I'm more experienced. I can deal with the art of travel now."

Nick Price: "I have a better understanding of my game and my swing. And my short game is twenty times better."

Colin Montgomerie: "Course management. I know when to play smarter, and I've learned a lot by watching other players compete."

Who has the best swing?

Tom Purtzer
Fred Couples
Steve Elkington
Gil Morgan
Rocco Mediate
Jeff Sluman
Nick Faldo
Larry Mize

And You Thought Being on the Cover of Sports Illustrated Was a Jinx?

Winning the U.S. Open in 1991 had a downside for Payne Stewart.

After he finished second and third on the money list the two previous years and copped the 1989 PGA Championship, everyone, including Stewart, assumed he was ready to rocket to the top of the golf world.

Instead, he dropped to forty-fourth on the money list in 1992—his lowest ranking since his rookie year of 1981. Part of the blame, he says, was winning the U.S. Open.

"It had an impact that wasn't entirely beneficial," he admits. "I asked advice from some people I trusted on what I could do to become even better. One of them said, 'Well, you need to be more structured in your daily routine, your practice routine, basically in your life.' So I tried that.

"I asked another person about my golf swing and he said, 'Well, if you'd take the loop out of your swing, you'd become more consistent.'

"I'm not a person who enjoys a lot of structure. I definitely found that out. And when I took the loop out of my swing, I lost all my feel. I became mechanical, and Payne Stewart is not a mechanical player. I'm a 'feel' player, and I've got to have that feel with my hands. I lost all of that."

In 1993, he dumped the routines and quit thinking about the mechanics of his game. So what happened? He finished sixth on the money list, earning over $980,000.

"I realized, 'You know, I'm a pretty decent player. Just go out and let your ability come through and quit trying to manufacture more ability than you have. The ability you have is pretty good. It can compete with anybody in the world.'"

Golf guru David Leadbetter says it would be a mistake to tamper with a swing as effective and unique as Stewart's.

"If there is a flaw in the swing that is continually causing problems, then you change it," said Leadbetter. "But golf is a game of compensations. For every flaw you make going back, you must make a correction going forward. As long as Payne continues to make a comparable compensation, he will always be a great player."

Says Stewart, "I'm just myself and I hope that's good enough. I've given up trying to be somebody else. I've found out what works for me. And what works for me is just being Payne Stewart."

If your game was at it best, how often would you win?

John Cook: "My game was at its best in 1992 [when he won three tournaments], so, three times."

Dave Stockton Jr.: "If my game was at its best, I think I could win a couple of times a year."

Dan Forsman: "Not often enough, goldang it. I could win out here, or should win, when I'm at my best at least one tournament out of every ten."

Scott Hoch: "When I'm playing my best, I ought to win one out of every four weeks. But I can't remember when it's been at its very best."

Ken Green: "Probably 25 percent of the time."

David Frost: "A good five or six times a year."

Mike Reid: "That might be a dangerous question to answer. I'd like to think I'm playing at my best every week, everywhere. That's part of the job description."

The Ten-Year Exemption

Nick Price—the leading money winner in 1993—says the pivotal date in his sterling career was the day he won the 1983 World Series of Golf.

It wasn't so much the title or the money. It was the other perk—a ten-year exemption on the Tour.

"Winning meant so much to me," Price said, "but more than anything, it meant that I could make the changes in my game that I needed to make and not have to worry about keeping my [Tour] card.

"People ask me, 'If your game was good enough to win the World Series, then why would you want to change?' I tell them, 'Because I only have that game two or three weeks a year.' I needed to develop a game that was consistent, day in and day out, week in and week out.

"A lot of guys will work on their golf swings on the practice tee and see improvement. Then they go out on the course during a tournament and chicken out. Instead of trying that new swing under pressure, they go back to the old one."

But with a ten-year exemption, he says, it makes a big difference because golfers are more likely to try that new swing.

Who are the best sand players?

Paul Azinger
Corey Pavin
David Frost
Mark Brooks
Ben Crenshaw
Bob Eastwood
Jack Nicklaus

What is the one part of your game you can bank on?

Fulton Allem: "My driving. Always."

Tom Kite: "I know my wedge game is always going to be good, but the one thing I count on more than anything else is Tom Kite. I just trust my ability to play."

Lee Janzen: "Over my entire career, it's been chipping. My putting is pretty strong, but sometimes it leaves me."

Joey Sindelar: "Generally speaking, it's hitting greens in regulation. I wouldn't label myself a great driver or iron player, but I can always count on hitting a fair amount of greens."

Ernie Els: "My bunker play. If I have a good lie, I'm not too bad out of the bunker."

Hal Sutton: "My irons are usually pretty reliable."

What is the least reliable part of your game?

Fulton Allem: "There really isn't one. I'm not scared off by any part of my game."

Tom Kite: "There are always things I need to work on."

Lee Janzen: "My long iron game, which I've almost eliminated. [Of the long irons] I only carry a three-iron, because I've got a four-wood and a lob wedge."

Joey Sindelar: "Chipping. I can't decide whether or not to putt-style my chips."

Ernie Els: "It's a toss-up between my putting and my driving."

Hal Sutton: "Probably my chipping."

Swing Thoughts

JC Andersen's secret to the perfect golf swing: "The pivot is the utilization of multiple centers to produce a circular motion for generating centrifugal force on an adjusted plane, plus the maintenance of balance necessary to promote the two-line delivery path."

Fred Couples, to the audience at a golf clinic: "As far as swing and techniques are concerned, I don't know diddly squat. When I'm playing well, I don't even take aim."

What rule or policy would you like to see changed?

Payne Stewart: "The spike mark rule. Say, for example, you're playing well and you hit a miraculous shot. You've got a four-foot, slippery slider down the hill. But, because of the rule, you don't have a chance to make it because someone has walked in front of you and left a spike mark. You should be allowed to tap that down. The rules-makers need to be big enough to realize the rule needs to be altered."

Bill Murchison: "Definitely the spike mark rule. The guy who tees off at seven in the morning plays a different golf course than a guy teeing off at 1:45 P.M.

"Also, I have seen some golf courses water the greens in the summer about one P.M. to keep them from drying out. But now you've changed the characteristics of the golf course. One group comes through and the greens are hard and dried out. Then the next group comes through and suddenly, they are wet and mushy. That's a policy that should be examined."

Donnie Hammond: "The one that says you can't wear shorts. That's more of a policy than a rule, but we need to be able to wear them in hot weather. Then again, if you ever saw Ed Fiori's or Leonard Thompson's legs, you'd understand why the rule is the way it is."

Gary Player: "I would like to see out of bounds as one penalty stroke. I think it's terribly unfair to have it at two shots. I don't like to build golf courses with out of bounds on both sides. I'm very much against that. When you have out of bounds on both sides, you ruin the hole."

David Peoples: "Definitely the one about keeping your score. You get disqualified if you screw up the score on your card. I think that's ridiculous. In every other major sport, people keep the score for you. The disqualification penalty is awfully severe. You could lose a major championship because you made a mistake on your card. It's happened before.

"If a guy is going to cheat, he's not going to do it on a scorecard. That's too obvious. Like somebody really thinks, 'I'm going to beat you because I'm writing down a three when I really had a four.' If you're going to cheat, you're going to go hit the ball deep into the woods and then put the ball up on a tee. You're not going to do anything so blatant as put down a wrong number on your card, especially when your playing partner is keeping your score also."

Mark McCumber: "The rule I'd like to change says you can't take a ball out of play once you've reached the green unless it is out of round. If I mark the ball and it is dirty, scuffed, or whatever, I have to bring a competitor over. He has to determine if it is out of round, and only then can I take it out. I think it would speed up play tremendously if you could switch your ball with one that's the same kind and same brand. You immediately pick up the ball you're playing with and switch with your caddie, so while he's cleaning the first ball, you can putt out with the other ball."

Brad Bryant: "I think you should be able to pick up your ball and take it out of a sand trap with a stroke penalty. Any place else on the golf course, if you get in a hazard, you have relief. But you can't get relief in a sand trap. I think that's crazy. It just doesn't make sense."

Ever since Nick Price won the
1992 PGA Championship, headlines in
newspapers and magazines that
run stories about him often proclaim,
"The Price is Right."
The phrase has become so overused
that Price jokes, "Maybe I should change
my name to Bob Barker."